The *Pervigilium Veneris*

Bloomsbury Latin Texts

The *Pervigilium Veneris*

A New Critical Text, Translation and Commentary

William M. Barton

BLOOMSBURY ACADEMIC
LONDON • NEW YORK • OXFORD • NEW DELHI • SYDNEY

BLOOMSBURY ACADEMIC
Bloomsbury Publishing Plc
50 Bedford Square, London, WC1B 3DP, UK
1385 Broadway, New York, NY 10018, USA

BLOOMSBURY, BLOOMSBURY ACADEMIC and the Diana logo
are trademarks of Bloomsbury Publishing Plc

First published in Great Britain 2018
Paperback edition first published 2020

Copyright © William M. Barton, 2018

A catalogue record for this book is available from the British Library.

Library of Congress Cataloging-in-Publication Data
Names: Barton, William M., editor, translator, writer of added commentary.
Title: The Pervigilium Veneris : a new critical text, translation and commentary /
William M. Barton.
Other titles: Pervigilium Veneris. Latin (Barton) | Container of (expression): Pervigilium
Veneris. Latin (Barton) | Container of (expression): Pervigilium Veneris. English (Barton)
Description: London ; New York : Bloomsbury Academic, 2018. | Text in Latin and English;
introduction and commentary in English. | Includes bibliographical references and index.
Identifiers: LCCN 2017049485 | ISBN 9781350040533 (hardback) |
ISBN 9781350040557 (epub)
Subjects: LCSH: Venus (Roman deity—Poetry. | LCGFT: Poetry.
Classification: LCC PA6557 .P3 2018 | DDC 871/.01—dc23 LC record available at
https://lccn.loc.gov/2017049485

ISBN: HB: 978-1-3500-4053-3
PB: 978-1-3501-3653-3
ePDF: 978-1-3500-4054-0
eBook: 978-1-3500-4055-7

Typeset by RefineCatch Limited, Bungay, Suffolk

To find out more about our authors and books visit
www.bloomsbury.com and sign up for our newsletters.

Contents

Acknowledgements

This book has had a long period of elaboration. I began my work on the *Pervigilium Veneris* while studying in the Department of Greek and Roman Studies at the University of Calgary, Canada between 2009 and 2011. My first words of thanks, then, must go to the faculty and my graduate school colleagues in Calgary who supported and encouraged my research, and made my stay in Alberta a real pleasure. In particular I am indebted to my supervisor in Calgary, Prof. Haijo Westra, who introduced me to the poem and oversaw my early work on the piece. Without the support of the Luke Bridgewater Memorial Scholarship from the department, the Dowager Countess Eleanor Peel Trust from Lancaster Royal Grammar School and a Teaching Assistantship, again from the University of Calgary, none of this initial study on the *Pervigilium* would have been possible.

After moving country (and into a new field of study) to complete a doctoral degree, I was able to come back to the *Pervigilium* during my work as a postdoctoral researcher at the Ludwig Boltzmann Institut für Neulateinische Studien (LBI) in Innsbruck, Austria. Returning to a previous area of research to develop and improve earlier work is a time-consuming process. I would like to acknowledge the patience and understanding of my colleagues at the LBI who allowed me to indulge my interest in this late antique poem while completing postdoctoral work on early modern Latin literature. In this context, the guidance of Prof. Martin Korenjak was especially helpful.

Finally, I would like to thank Alice Wright at Bloomsbury Academic whose patience and belief in this project has been very valuable, the anonymous reviewers of an earlier version of this edition whose comments, corrections and criticisms were enormously constructive in the later stages of work, and the reviewers of the original edition of this book before March 2019 (especially D. Libatique *CR* Oct. 2018 pp. 1–3), whose comments have helped bring the study to its current form

Note on the Latin Text

The *Pervigilium Veneris* has attracted the attention of many and various scholars since its rediscovery by Aldus Manutius or Erasmus in 1507 and its *editio princeps* by Pierre Pithou in 1578. The sheer number of scholarly works on the piece up to 1936 was demonstrated in Clementi's extensive bibliography to his luxurious *variorum* edition.[1] The briefest inquiry with any of today's electronic research tools will reveal that interest in the poem has not dwindled, indeed it has perhaps increased since Clementi's work.

'The criticism of certain works of literature sometimes develops a life of its own.'[2] It is with this in mind that the reader might approach the stout *apparatus* to be found at the foot of the text. It has been with a keen and interested eye on the layers of scholarship which have preserved, transmitted and informed our understanding of this piece that I have compiled the critical *apparatus*, recording the important, interesting and also remarkable readings which make up the history of the poem and its meaning to its numerous readers over the centuries.

In cases where mere orthographical variants are present in the manuscripts, I have decided to include them in the *apparatus* because they have often been pertinent to resolving corrupt readings elsewhere in the text. This is the case, for example, with the frequent confusion of the voiced and unvoiced dental consonants in MS S. For lines

---

[1]   C. Clementi, 1936. *Pervigilium Veneris, The Vigil of Venus. Edited with Facsimiles of the Codex Salmasianus, Codex Thuaneus and Codex Sannazarii: An Introduction, Translation, Apparatus Criticus, Bibliography and Explanatory Notes* (Oxford: Blackwell and Mott), 94–164.

[2]   H. MacL. Currie, 1993. 'Pervigilium Veneris' in *Aufstieg und Niedergang der römischen Welt Teil II: Principat*, 34 (1) ed. W. Haase and H. Temporini (Berlin: De Gruyter, 1993), 207.

where corruption has sparked particularly prolific conjecture I have included the important, interesting and frequently adopted emendations in order to evidence the sheer level of attention that this poem has received and the variety of ideas that such attention has inspired.

List of Abbreviations

AC   *Agadiorum chiliades tres*

AL   *Anthologia Latina*

HLL   *Handbuch der lateinischen Literatur der Antike*

OLD   *Oxford Latin Dictionary*

TLL   *Thesaurus Linguae Latinae*

Introduction

Since its first edition in 1578 by Pierre Pithou, the *Pervigilium Veneris* has at once bewildered and enchanted readers and editors alike. The poem of ninety-three trochaic tetrameter verses is of uncertain authorship and date. It is preserved in only four heavily corrupt manuscripts. On the surface, the piece presents itself as a literary hymn to the goddess of love, Venus. The scene is set in spring on the island of Sicily in the proverbially lush landscape surrounding the town of Hybla, where a three-day festival is taking place in honour of the goddess:

> Detinenda tota nox est, pervigilanda canticis!

Nymphs, the Graces, Ceres, Bacchus, Apollo, and Venus's son Cupid all attend this vernal festival in celebration of Venus's birth, her role in nature's renewal, and her traditional association with the Roman people. The events, over which Venus presides, will also celebrate the blossoming of maidens into women through the ritual of marriage. In this sense the poem is also an epithalamium. But contributing to the mystery and allure of the piece, its final stanza introduces an enigmatic twist when, in the midst of a final pastoral scene, the author himself steps into the poem and addresses the reader to reveal his own internal plight.

The *Pervigilium* is divided into self-contained and uneven stanzas by a refrain that appropriately appeals for universal love:

> Cras amet qui numquam amavit, quique amavit cras amet!

Along with the various and often passionately argued proposals for the date, authorship, and resolution of issues in the manuscript tradition, the refrain and the division of stanzas have been key points of contention within the modern scholarship on the *Pervigilium*. This edition of the poem will advance previous scholarship with new evidence and proposals for many of these central topics while building upon and reviving valuable ideas forgotten or dismissed.

The Manuscript Tradition

Four manuscripts preserve the *Pervigilium Veneris*, all of which derive from a single archetype.[1] The oldest of these is the Codex Salmasianus Parisinus 10318, so named for its discovery by the French scholar Claude de Saumaise in 1615.[2] Preserved on folios 108–12, the poem is written in a single column in an uncial script. One proposal dates the manuscript to the seventh century and makes it the work of a Spanish scribe.[3] But a more detailed argument, commonly accepted in recent scholarship, places it at the end of the eighth century and proposes an Italian origin.[4] The poem is prefaced by a short inscription in this manuscript, which reads:

INCIPIT · PER · VIRGILIUM · VENERIS · TROCHAICO · METRO · Sunt vero versus XXII

After considerable confusion over the meaning of the phrase *Sunt vero versus XXII*, Riese saw in 1869 that the figure refers to the number of poems contained in the section of the *Anthologia Latina* beginning

1   L. Catlow, 'Pervigilium Veneris', *Latomus revue d'études latines*, 172 (Brussels: Latomus, 1980), 7. See also the manuscript stemma below.
2   C. Clementi, *Pervigilium Veneris, The Vigil of Venus. Edited with Facsimiles of the Codex Salmasianus, Codex Thuaneus and Codex Sannazarii: An Introduction, Translation, Apparatus Criticus, Bibliography and Explanatory Notes,* 3rd edn (Oxford: Blackwell and Mott, 1936), 26–7.
3   L. Traube, 'Zur lateinischen Anthologie', *Philologus* 54 (1895), 124.
4   B. Bischoff, 'Panorama der Handschriftenüberlieferung aus der Zeit Karls des Grossen', in *Karl der Grosse: Lebenswerk und Nachleben,* ed. W. Braunfels and H. Beumann, 5 vols, vol. 2 (Düsseldorf: L. Schwann, 1965), 249 and 253.

with the *Pervigilium*.[5] The collection of poems recorded in the Codex Salmasianus was compiled around the beginning of the sixth century A.D. in Carthage for one of the last Vandal kings of the city.[6] Not only is the Salmasianus (S) the oldest of the four manuscripts, it is also one of the most important for the text of the *Pervigilium* since it represents a branch of the tradition independent from that to which the codices Thuaneus (T), Vindobonensis (V), and Ambrosianus (A) belong. The evidence for this independence can be found at lines eleven, seventeen, and twenty-three, for example, where TVA agree in error against S, and lines seven and thirty-eight where S contains an error which is absent from TVA. S has the correct reading at lines fifty-five, sixty-two, sixty-nine, seventy-eight, eighty-two, eighty-six, and eighty-seven where TV err, and TV are correct at sixty-two, eighty-five, and ninety-one, for example, against S.[7]

Codex Parisinus 8071 'Thuaneus' is the second oldest manuscript, although it was the first discovered. It dates from the end of the ninth or the start of the tenth century and originated from France in the region of Orléans, possibly at the Abbey of Fleury.[8] It was from this manuscript alone that Pierre Pithou produced his *editio princeps*.[9] On account of this connection the codex is sometimes also referred to as the *Pithoeanus*. The *Pervigilium* is preserved on folio fifty-two

---

[5]   A. Riese, *Anthologia Latina I, Libri Salmasiani aliorumque carmina*, 2nd edn (Leipzig: Teubner [1869], repr. 1894). Indeed, the confusion was prolonged even after Riese's solution of the mystery: see J. A. Fort, *The Pervigilium Veneris in Quatrains* (London; Oxford: Humphrey Milford; Oxford University Press, 1922), who, for example, took the inscription to mean that the poem ought to have 22 verses and accordingly divided up the poem into equal stanzas of four lines separated by the refrain. He even goes as far as to add five lines to the poem to make the verses even. Two of these extra verses were penned by J. W. Mackail and the remainder by himself.
[6]   F. M. Clover, 'Felix Karthago', *Dumbarton Oaks Papers* 40 (1986), 1–16.
[7]   The copy of the *Pervigilium* in the Codex Ambrosianus cuts off after the first word of line 43. See below for a more detailed discussion of this MS.
[8]   F. P. Capponi, *Ovidii Nasonis Halieuticon Volume I – Introduzione e Testo*, 2 vols, vol. 1 (Leiden: E. J. Brill, 1972), 169.
[9]   On the *editio princeps* of the *Pervigilium* see H. Omont, 'Sur le Pervigilium Veneris, I. Conjectures de Joseph Scaliger', *Revue de Philologie* 9 (1885), 124–6.

in a Carolingian minuscule hand. The text is copied in two parallel columns with regular spacing between the words. The relationship of the Thuaneus (T) to manuscripts V and A is proven by their common readings against the Salmasianus listed above. Within the TVA branch, T can be shown to be more closely related to A by common errors in lines three, nine, ten, fifteen, and thirty-two where V preserves the correct readings with S. Moreover, line forty, which is missing from T, is also absent from A, whereas in V it is intact.

In 1867 Karl Schenkl discovered that the Codex Vindobonensis 9401 contained the *Pervigilium,* and since then scholars have contested its importance as a witness to the poem.[10] It has been demonstrated that the humanist hand in which the poem is copied is the autograph of Italian poet Jacopo Sannazaro, but discussion has centred upon the manuscript from which Sannazaro copied the poem.[11] Some early editors believed that the Vindobonensis was copied directly from the Thuaneus (Parisinus 8071). Baehrens, for example, writes on the matter: 'ex T fluxerunt epigrammata quaedam vetusta ab Actio Sincerio [*sic*] Sannazario exscripta in codice Vindobonensi lat. 9041 [*sic*]'.[12] But the accuracy of V, especially in lines nine and ten and the preservation of line forty, quickly helped later editors to realize the importance of V as an independent witness for the poem. Clementi collected evidence to demonstrate that V agrees to a large extent with S, both in errors and in correct readings, but most interestingly that V, S, and T all agree in striking errors,

[10] K. Schenkl, 'Zur Kritik des Pervigilium Veneris', *Zeitschrift für die österreichischen Gymnasien* 18 (1867), 233–43.
[11] C. Clementi, *Pervigilium Veneris, The Vigil of Venus*: 44–5 and R. Schilling, *La Veillée de Vénus. Pervigilium Veneris* (Paris: Les Belles Lettres, 1944), lxi.
[12] A. Baehrens, *Poetae Latini Minores Volumen IV* (Leipzig: Teubner, 1882), 9. The error in citing the codex as 9041 instead of 9401 began with Schenkl, as pointed out in Catlow, *Pervigilium Veneris*, 8. It was prolonged by Riese who cited Baehrens in the introduction to his edition of the *Anthologia Latina*: Riese, *Anthologia Latina I,* 2nd edn, xxvii, where he expresses the same opinion on the origins of codex V.

for instance on lines fifty and eighty-one. Critical for establishing the independent value of codex V was the discovery that V has correct readings where S and T err; in particular lines two, fifty-two, and sixty-two.[13] Clementi thus came to the conclusion that Sannazaro had made his copy of the text from a manuscript – now lost – which represented an earlier part of the tradition than T. This is also the conclusion of Catlow, who dismisses the alternative theories attempting to explain V's accuracy.[14] Such alternative explanations of V's correct readings were suggested, for example, by Cazzaniga (1959), who proposed that V did indeed descend from T but that Sannazaro had access to another manuscript from the same family as S with which he corrected his copy,[15] and Schilling, who argued that V's accuracy derives largely from Sannazarian conjecture.[16]

Cazzaniga's view is unlikely because if Sannazaro had indeed had access to a manuscript from the S family and used it to correct errors such as those in lines nine and ten and the reinsertion of line forty, he would surely also have corrected the errors of T in lines eleven, seventeen, or ninety-one, for example, which he merely copied. Schilling's conclusion that Sannazaro corrected the T tradition through conjecture is not viable because more complicated errors were corrected, such as on lines twenty-six, sixty-one and eighty-six, when less complex errors such as on lines eleven, twenty-nine, and eighty-two, were simply repeated. Furthermore, while V does make some slips of its own which do not appear in S or T in lines thirty-one and sixty-seven, for example, the 'emendation' that Schilling proposes

---

[13] Clementi, *Pervigilium Veneris, The Vigil of Venus*, 44–7.
[14] Catlow, *Pervigilium Veneris*, 8–10, without reference to Clementi.
[15] I. Cazzaniga, *Carmina Ludicra Romanorum: Pervigilium – Priapea* (Turin: G. B. Paravia, 1959), vii. *Reliquos contra codices ex T vel recta vel obliqua derivatos esse putamus, ut V, in quo Sannazarius lectiones contulit paucas (quas ex codice S non recta via, tamen fortasse per litteras putes deprompsisse).*
[16] Schilling, *La Veillée de Vénus*, lxi–lxii.

does not appear to have introduced any spurious readings into the text through misinterpretation. Scaliger and Pithou, working only from T, managed to resolve many errors such as *casas* from *gazas* in line six and *praeses* from *praesens* in line fifty-one, but they also further corrupted the text in places where an emendation could not be made, such as in line nine where, from *quiuore* in T, Pithou reads *qui rore* and Scaliger *liquore*. Here SV transmit the correct reading *cruore*. A similar case occurs in Scaliger's emendation and re-interpretation of lines twenty-two and twenty-three: he reads *ludant* for *nubant*, places a full stop before *rosae*, reads T *fusta* as *fusae* and changes *Amoris* to *Adonis*. It is improbable that Sannazaro could have made so many accurate corrections without making any serious blunders.

The codex Vindobonensis also contains alternative readings and corrections in the margins. These, as has been convincingly argued, are Sannazaro's emendations which he noted while transcribing the text.[17] Following this view, the emendations have been noted as Sannazarian scholarship in the *apparatus criticus*.[18] Sannazaro marked his sensible conjectures with the symbol '*f.*' in the margin.[19] He offers, for example, *osculis* for *oculis* at line twenty-three and *annus* for *annis* at line fifty-two, whereas he leaves the troublesome line seventeen alone without any indication of an attempt to better it. Sannazaro's fidelity as a copyist and his scrupulousness in recording his changes is indicated by his efforts to record his emendation *posuit* for *possuit* on line thirty-one and *iussitque* for *iusitque* on line sixty-seven, both of which could have been quite confidently made

---

17   Clementi, *Pervigilium Veneris, The Vigil of Venus*, 46; Catlow, *Pervigilium Veneris*, 11–12.
18   Except *posuit* for *possuit* on line thirty-one and *iussitque* for *iusitque* on line sixty-seven, which are simply orthographical corrections.
19   Clementi, *Pervigilium Veneris, The Vigil of Venus*, 46 suggests that *f.* stands for *forte*. Catlow, *Pervigilium Veneris*, 11–12 proposes *fortasse*, while Schilling thinks *fiat*.

without much hesitation for thought, let alone recording. Moreover, Sannazaro went to the trouble of recording some readings above the line which he surely cannot have thought to have been preferable to those in his text: *unicat* above *unica* in line twenty-six for example. In addition, he records two equally meaningless readings at line twenty-three for *facta*: *fusta* and *furta*. Catlow saw that these interlinear additions are instances of Sannazaro recording the original versions of the manuscripts. Where a word is underlined without a marginal note, as in *latino* line sixty-nine and *ta onii* line eighty-one, Clementi realized that Sannazaro was identifying a word for which no emendation seemed apparent to him. Several lines have next to them the *signe de renvoi* '+' which appears to indicate that an error occurs in the line.[20] The notations made by Sannazaro in his copying of the text serve to underline the importance of the codex Vindobonensis as evidence for the transmission of the poem, regardless of its relative youth in comparison to S and T.

In contrast, the codex Ambrosianus sup. 81 is a descendant of T which is intermittently subjected to unrecorded humanist conjecture.[21] A agrees with V in numerous places against T: on lines one to five, eight, thirteen, sixteen to nineteen, twenty to twenty-two, twenty-four, twenty-eight, thirty-three, thirty-six, thirty-eight, thirty-nine and forty-one. In each case these agreements are attributable to emendation of an obvious error, for example, at line thirteen where T has *gemmas* for VA *gemmis,* or at line thirty-eight where T has *re* and VA agree on *res.* When A comes up against a serious problem in T, however, it reveals its close relationship with its ancestor: on

---

[20] In lines nine, fifteen, seventeen, twenty-three, forty-five, fifty-one, fifty-two, fifty-five, fifty-eight, eighty-one, eighty-two, eighty-three, eighty-seven, ninety and ninety-one (listed by Clementi, *Pervigilium Veneris, The Vigil of Venus*, 46).

[21] Catlow, *Pervigilium Veneris*, 14–15.

line nine where T has *quivore* (*cruore* SV), A tries to make sense of
T's text but falls short with *qui vere*. Similarly, on line seventeen
T transmits *decadum* (*de caduco* S) from which A produces *dea dum*.
In another comparable example T muddles both the sense and meter
in recording *pudent solvere* for *pudebit solvere* SV; here A attempts to
correct T's errors with *pudet dissolvere*. Significantly, A also omits line
forty following T. This line's inclusion was evidence that V represents
an earlier branch of the tradition than T and it is difficult not to see it
as proof of A's direct relationship to T.

In 1998, Formicola proposed that 'l'omissione del 40 può essere
interpretato come errore poligenetico, spiegabile con un banale "saut
du même au même"'.[22] However, in the absence of external evidence,
A's 'corrections' of what must have been T's text (*quivore* T with *qui
vere* A or *decadum* T with *dea dum* A), as well as the omission of
line forty, stack the evidence in favour of the argument that A is a
descriptus of T. In places where the copyist of A came upon words
too corrupt for him to manage, he reveals the direct relationship of
his copy to T with his unsuccessful emendations. In view of these
arguments, I have not included the readings of A in my apparatus.
Those editors who do record A's readings, as in the case of Formicola,
recognize that it contributes nothing substantive to our knowledge
of the text.[23]

In his review of Clementi's third edition of the *Pervigilium*, Rand
prepared the following *stemma codicum* for the text.[24] I have added to
Rand's *stemma* the position of the codex Ambrosianus, indicating
Formicola's *caveat* that A may be indirectly descended from T:

[22] C. Formicola, *Pervigilium Veneris* (Naples: Loffredo Editore, 1998), 23. Formicola has
      this as part of his argument that A derives from T but by an indirect route: *ibid.* 22–4.
[23] '[A] non fornisce nessun apporto alla constituzione del testo' Formicola, *Pervigilium
      Veneris*, 22.
[24] E. K. Rand, Review: 'Pervigilium Veneris by C. Clementi', *The American Journal of
      Philology* 58, no. 4 (1937), 474–8.

Stemma Codicum

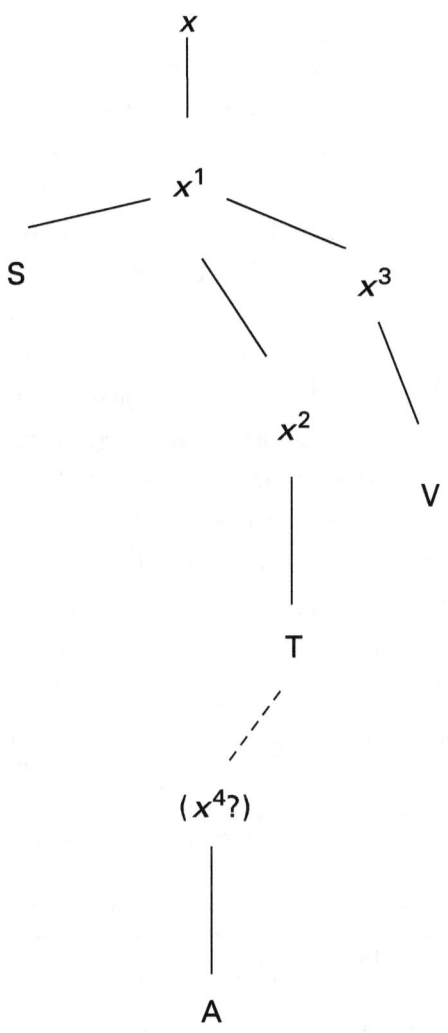

Date and Authorship

Of the many and varied candidates proposed by modern studies for the authorship of the *Pervigilium* none has been outside of the post-classical period.[25] When the more fantastic suggestions are cleared from the table,[26] the scholarship falls into roughly two groups, one of which favours a second century date and the other a fourth or early fifth. A number of scholars have used the eighth stanza – particularly line seventy-four – as basis for their proposals of date and authorship.[27] P. S. Davies' solution of what Catlow thought to be line seventy-four's 'insoluble crux',[28] which is adopted in my text and defended in the notes on that line, shows that stanza eight is dedicated to recounting the mytho-historical connection of Venus to Rome.[29] Line seventy-four simply concludes the logical and chronological progression from the Goddess's role in the blending of the Trojan and Latin lines (line sixty-nine) to her position at the head of the *gens Iulia*. With this in mind, those candidates for authorship whose claim

---

[25] Catlow, *Pervigilium Veneris*, 18. The poem was linked to a classical author in Erasmus's *Adagia*: *Meminit et Catullus, nisi fallit inscriptio carminis De Vere, quod nuper nobis Albus Manutius meus exhibuit . . . (AC* 809) (Erasmus, D. *Adagiorum chiliades tres, ac centuriae fere totidem* (Basle: J. Froben, 1517)).
Here the humanist's doubt over the purported Catullan authorship of the poem is obvious.

[26] Listed by Catlow, *Pervigilium Veneris*, 18 n. 2 and as part of Clementi's review (pp. 75–90) of all the date and authorship proposals. A good overview of the various proposals for the poem's authorship, as well as its interpretation, after Clementi is C. Condoñer, 'On the One and the Diverse: Pervigilium Veneris', in *New Perspectives on Late Antiquity*, ed. D. Hernández de la Fuente (Newcastle: Cambridge Scholars Publishing, 2011), 263–87.

[27] Notably D. S. Robertson, 'The Date and Occasion of the Pervigilium Veneris', *The Classical Review* 52, no. 3 (1938), 109–12 who worked from the phrase *Romuli matrem* in line 74 and came up with a date of 307 A.D. and authorship by a poet at the court of the emperor C. Galerius Valerius Maximianus. Also E. K. Rand, 'Sur le *Pervigilium Veneris*', *Revue des études latines* 12 (1934b), 82–95 who, from the same starting point, arrived at a date between the years 138–61 A.D.. The attempts at dating using line 74 have been listed by Clementi, *Pervigilium Veneris, The Vigil of Venus*, 78–82.

[28] *Romu(o)li matrem* STV Catlow, *Pervigilium Veneris*, 87. Davies reads *Iulium* with Scaliger's *mater*.

[29] P. S. Davies, 'The Text of Pervigilium Veneris 74', *The Classical Quarterly* 42, no. 2 (1992), 575–7.

depends on an argument construed from line seventy-four are dismissed.

Scholars who have settled upon the second century date have regarded the *Pervigilium* as a testimony to the revival of the cult of *Venus Genetrix* which occurred under the emperor Hadrian and which was marked by the dedication of a temple to Venus on 21 April 128 A.D.[30] Indeed, the *Pervigilium* has been directly associated with a trip that Hadrian made to Sicily.[31] P. Boyancé even goes as far as to suggest that the piece may have been written as a chorus to be sung during a night procession of the sort described in the poem itself, reflecting the emperor's visit to and interest in Sicily.[32] In a similar vein, Cazzaniga argues that the poem was written for a local Sicilian festival connected to one of the ancient towns of Hybla.[33]

In contrast, other scholars have seen the poem as unconnected to any actual ritual or festival whatsoever, but rather as a 'motive of fantasy'.[34] More recently, and most convincingly, Catlow has argued that although the festival in the poem may well have its roots in historical *pervigilia* and similar festivals, the poem takes this simply as a literary and inspirational setting rather than describing actual celebrations.[35] The work does not have any of the features of a genuine liturgical chant such as Horace's *Carmen Saeculare*, for example.

---

[30] R. Schilling, *La Veillée de Vénus*, xxiv–xxv.
[31] The island forms the backdrop in which the *Pervigilium* is set (lines fifty to fifty-three). See note on line fifty for my argument, after Catlow, that the Sicilian setting serves to situate the poem in the proverbially lush landscape of Latin literature rather than in an actual geographical location.
[32] P. Boyancé, 'Le "Pervigilium Veneris" et les "veneralia"', *Publications de l'École française de Rome* 11, no. 1 (1972), 383–99.
[33] I. Cazzaniga, 'Saggio critico ed esegetico sul Pervigilium Veneris', *Studi classici e orientali* 3 (1955), 47–63. See note below on line fifty for the argument against connecting the poem with a precise historical and geographical location and taking the reference to Hybla as a call to the classical literary tradition of the lush Sicilian landscape.
[34] J. W. Mackail, *Catullus, Tibullus and the Pervigilium Veneris* (Cambridge, Massachusetts; London: Harvard University Press; William Heinemann, 1913), 345.
[35] See: Catlow, *Pervigilium Veneris*, 26–35 for his detailed discussion.

Boyancé suggests that the poem might have had a female author,[36] a proposal which Catlow takes up while himself deciding on a fourth century date.[37] Boyancé draws his evidence from the fact that the *pervigilia* as festivals were most often associated with women and that in the poem the only named worshippers at the festival are the nymphs.[38] Even at this basic level of his argument there is room to challenge its assertions, for it is not hard to imagine why *pervigilia*, mainly attended by women, would be the subject of a love poem written by a man. Moreover, the appearance of the male gods Bacchus, Apollo[39] and Cupid[40] complicates Boyancé's female-only setting. And if gods are somehow above the sex restrictions for this festival why, then, is Diana required to leave her forest during the course of the poem?[41] Even Catlow, writing in favour of attributing the poem to female authorship, calls the French scholar's comparisons between Sappho's poetry and the *Pervigilium* 'largely chimerical.'[42]

The support which Catlow adduces for his expansion of Boyancé's suggestion of female authorship does little to aid the cause. He relies on the evidence that *nubunt* in line three shows that the poet intended to equate the birds with brides, and that the *nemus* of line four is personified as a woman.[43] Catlow's argument is perhaps strongest as he turns to the interpretation of the final stanza,[44] in particular lines eighty-six to ninety, where he suggests that because the poet compares himself to the swallow, a female in myth,[45] 'this emphasis, in a context so intimately bound up with the deepest longings of

[36]   P. Boyancé, 'Encore le Pervigilium Veneris', *Revue des études latines*, 28 (1950), 232.
[37]   Catlow, *Pervigilium Veneris*, 24–5.
[38]   Boyancé, 'Encore le Pervigilium Veneris', 218.
[39]   Line forty six: *Nec Ceres, nec Bacchus absunt nec poetarum deus.*
[40]   Line twenty-nine: *It puer comes puellis . . .*
[41]   Line thirty-eight: *Una res est quam rogamus: cede virgo Delia.*
[42]   The 'chimerical' comparions to Sappho are made at Boyancé, 'Encore le Pervigilium Veneris', 218–19, and criticized by Catlow, *The Pervigilium Veneris*, 24.
[43]   See note on line 4 for my more polyvalent interpretation of this image.
[44]   Catlow, *The Pervigilium Veneris*, 25.
[45]   See below notes on lines eighty-six to ninety-four.

the poet, betokens, ... the feelings and imaginative response of a woman'.[46] However, my interpretation of the final stanza,[47] based on a close reading of what internal evidence the text itself furnishes, proposes that the poet intends the swallow as a symbol of ambiguity – not femininity – and that whereas longings, desires and love are certainly a part of the poem's fabric, the poet's loss of song and reaction to the spring scenery says more about his sudden self-awareness and self-consciousness than anything about his gender.

Within the second century the candidate most frequently forwarded for authorship of the *Pervigilium* is Florus,[48] who was both a historian and poet under the emperor Hadrian.[49] Florus's poems survive in the *Anthologia Latina*.[50] One of them is composed on the subject of a rose and another eight pieces are written in trochaic tetrameter catalectic.[51] The similarities between Florus's *œuvre* and the *Pervigilium Veneris* end here, however, and are not as solid as they superficially appear. Of the two manuscripts which contain poems *AL* 238–45, the Salmasianus and the Thuaneus, only the first attributes them to Florus (the Thuaneus credits a mysterious 'Floridus' with the verses). The metrical practices of this 'Florus' are also quite out of keeping with the *Pervigilium*: Florus has three quadrisyllabic line endings in twenty-six lines compared to the *Pervigilium*'s one in ninety-three lines (*silentium* line ninety-two); Florus frequently elides, whereas this only occurs in the *Pervigilium* in the refrain; Florus makes liberal use of resolution of trochees into tribrachs, which only occurs once in the *Pervigilum* in line thirty-one (*posuit*). Finally, at a more general level the poems attributed to Florus are of a much shorter length and lesser quality than the *Pervigilium*.

---

[46] Catlow, *The Pervigilium Veneris*, 25.
[47] See the subchapter 'The Final Stanza and Interpretation of the Poem' below.
[48] See for example R. Schilling, *La Veillée de Vénus*, xxii–xxxii.
[49] Rand, 'Sur le Pervigilium Veneris', 93.
[50] *AL* 238–45 grouped under the heading *De qualitate vitae*.
[51] For the meter of the *Pervigilium*, refer to the following section 'The Meter' for further detail.

The very choice of the trochaic tetrameter catalectic sets the *Pervigilium* in the period of rediscovery of this meter, which was largely overlooked by classical authors.[52] The meter saw much more extended use in the early fourth century with Prudentius, Hilary of Poitiers and Tiberianus.[53] With these doubts over Florus's claim to authorship of the *Pervigilium*, it is to the fourth century that scholars have next looked to find the author and historical setting of the poem.

C. Brakman collected verbal evidence to show that the *Pervigilium* was most likely written in the fourth century. He takes as evidence the use of *vel* as alternative for *et* in line fifty-four,[54] the frequent use of the *praesens pro futuro* (see, for example, line seven), the lengthened third syllable of *Romuleas* in line seventy-two, the use of the post-classical *congrex* in line forty-three and the frequent employment of the preposition *de* throughout the poem.[55] Much of Brakman's evidence has been refuted by later scholarship,[56] and his suggestion to look within the circle of the pagan Quintus Aurelius Symmachus for a candidate for authorship has only received limited support from W. Rollo.[57] Within this circle Rollo proposed V. Nicomachus Flavianus as the poem's author, and later L. Herrmann brought forward the name of Claudius Antonius.[58] Catlow argues convincingly that our search should be directed away from the Symmachean literary circle,

---

[52] A. Cameron, 'The Pervigilium Veneris', *La poesia tardoantica: tra retorica, teologia e politica*. Atti del V Corso della Scuola Superiore di Archeologia e Civiltà Medievali (Messina: Università degli studi di Messina, Centro di studi umanistici, 1984), 218.

[53] Cameron, *The Pervigilium Veneris*, 217.

[54] See note below for my slightly different interpretation of this word in this line and the importance of the subtlety in meaning with the same word in line ninety.

[55] C. Brakman, 'Quando Pervigilium Veneris conditum est?' *Mnemosyne* 56 (1928), 254–70.

[56] *Vel* for *et* is known from the classical period and *congrex* is found in Apuleius (Catlow, *Pervigilium Veneris*, 20), *de* is taken by Cameron (*The Pervigilium Veneris*, 215) as a stylistic feature of the poem rather than a late antique usage.

[57] Brakman proposes Symmachus's circle in 'Quando Pervigilium Veneris conditum est?' 260–1. Rollo takes this up in W. Rollo, 'The Date and Authorship of the Pervigilium Veneris', *Classical Philology* 24, no. 4 (1929), 405–8.

[58] L. Hermann, 'Claudius Antonius et le Pervigilium Veneris', *Latomus revue d'études latines*, 12 (Brussels: Latomus, 1953), 53–69.

but it was Brakman's study which helped to cultivate the now more commonly held opinion that the poem belongs to the fourth century.[59]

Cameron's forcefully argued study renews the old proposal of A. Baehrens that Tiberianus wrote the *Pervigilium*.[60] There are a number of men by the name of Tiberianus who have been identified as the author of several poems dating from the fourth century. Traditionally, Annius Tiberianus – mentioned in Jerome's chronicle as a *vir disertus*, an official in Africa in 326 A.D., in Spain in 332 A.D. and governor of Gaul in 335 A.D. – has been credited with the poems.[61] But Cameron would also consider Iunius Tiberianus, who was prefect of Rome in 303–4 A.D., or his father of the same name.[62] Cameron arrives at a Tiberianus in the early fourth century following the evidence that he adduces on the grounds of 1) the poem's literary models; the poet uses images and ideas from Silver Age poets[63] – interest in the Silver Age poets was revived in the fourth century after having fallen out of favour in the second and third centuries;[64] 2) the poem's meter and metrical technique – the trochaic tetrameter catalectic (see subchapter on the meter below) experienced a brief renaissance in the fourth century; 3) the style of the poem, which matches up with features of Tiberianus's other poems. On the topic of style, Tiberianus's *Amnis ibat* shares with the *Pervigilium* certain interesting features, such as the rare adjective *musico* (line eighty-seven in the *Pervigilium*), an appeal to the reader's imagination towards the end of the poem with the word *putes* (also line eighty-seven in the *Pervigilium*):

[59] Catlow, *Pervigilium Veneris*, 23–4.
[60] Baehrens, *Poetae Latini Minores IV*, 48.
[61] J. W. Duff and A. M. Duff, *Minor Latin Poets* (London: William Heinemann, 1935). The Loeb edition contains the four poems attributed to Tiberianus as well as his collected fragments.
[62] Cameron, *The Pervigilium Veneris*, 225.
[63] See line twenty's *astra rorant* from Statius, *Thebaid 5*.
[64] Cameron, *The Pervigilium Veneris*, 215.

Has per umbras omnis ales plus canora quam putes

Cantibus vernis strepebat et susurris dulcibus[65]

as well as the strikingly similar image of the *nemus rigidum* (line thirty-nine of the *Pervigilium*):[66]

Roscidum nemus rigebat inter uda gramina.[67]

Affinities of metrical style also exist between the *Pervigilium* and Tiberianus's trochaic *Amnis ibat*, notably the admission of fifth foot spondees, which appear in the *Pervigilium* at lines fifty (/ *adsed* / *erunt*) and sixty (/ *vernis* /) for example,[68] and in the *Amnis* at lines six (/ *et lu* / *cebat*) and fourteen (/ *guttis* /). The *Amnis*, like the *Pervigilium*, also avoids quadrisyllables at the end of the line. They never appear in the former and only once in the latter (line ninety-two *silentium*). Added to this is the use of parallelism, in both the form of the rhyme and the structure of the line, which occurs both in the *Amnis* and the *Pervigilium*.[69] In the *Amnis* rhyme is found within the line on verse nineteen, and consecutively between lines ten and eleven and between sixteen and seventeen.[70] In the *Pervigilium*, line three presents the first example; see the note on this line for further examples of internal and consecutive rhyme.

Cameron devotes a considerable part of his paper to showing that Tiberianus was well acquainted with Greek philosophical thought, in particular the Neo-Platonists Plotinus and Porphyry.[71] Tiberianus wrote a poem in hexameters which takes the form of a hymn to the Platonists' Supreme God.[72] Of the five manuscripts which preserve

[65] Tiberianus, 1.15–16. The text of the *Amnis Ibat* is reproduced in the Appendix below.
[66] Moved from its position at line fifty-eight in the MSS in my text following Cameron and Catlow. See note to this line below for the reasoning behind this move.
[67] Tiberianus, 1.11.
[68] Catlow, *Pervigilium Veneris*, 36.
[69] H. MacL. Currie, 'Pervigilium Veneris', *Aufstieg und Niedergang der römischen Welt* II, 34, 1 (Berlin, New York: Walter de Gruyter, 1993), 215–20 and n. 31.
[70] For an interesting parallel patterning of consecutive rhyme see lines 1–4 of the *Amnis Ibat* with the pattern A–B–A–B.
[71] Cameron, *The Pervigilium Veneris*, 222–6.
[72] Appendix item 2.

the poem, two inform us that the poem is *versus Platonis a quodam Tiberiano de greco in latini translati,* another simply ascribes it directly to Plato. The poem of thirty-two lines concentrates on the four main topics of Plato's *Timaeus* and shows itself to be a well informed and serious piece most likely translating a hymn from Porphyry's *Philosophy of the Oracles.*[73] I have argued in the commentary to the text,[74] that the Stoic allusions seen in the *Pervigilium* by previous editors serve no other purpose than to give a philosophical flavour to the seventh stanza which concerns Venus's role in the creation of the world and continuing re-creation within it.[75] However, it is my belief that the change in tone in the enigmatic and arresting final stanza has a broadly philosophical motivation and it is certainly pertinent that the philosophical tradition to which the poet's perspective in the final stanza has been traced is Neo-Platonic.[76] In bringing together these observations on the philosophical influences present in the *Omnipotens* (*Hymn to the Supreme Being*), and hinted at in the *Pervigilium,* as well as the considerations of date, style and meter, it seems to me *probable* that Tiberianus can be credited with the authorship of the *Pervigilium Veneris,* although in the absence of any external evidence to back this up it is unlikely that the question over the date and authorship of the piece can ever be definitively solved.

Indeed, Tiberianus's sound claim to authorship has met with strong resistance. D. Shanzer sought to show that the *Pervigilium* has a *terminus post quem* of 368 A.D.[77] And Catlow has argued that the

---

[73] H. Lewy, 'A Latin Hymn to the Creator Ascribed to Plato', *The Harvard Theological Review* 39, no. 4 (1946), 243–58.

[74] See note on line sixty-three below.

[75] Editors who have emphasized the Stoic flavour of the *Pervigilium* include Clementi, *Pervigilium Veneris, The Vigil of Venus,* 204 and R. Schilling, *La Veillée de Vénus,* 13, for example. The Stoic ideas noted in Tiberianus's piece on the supreme god which have been blended into the Platonic background of the poem (Lewy, 'A Latin Hymn to the Creator ascribed to Plato', 255) parallel this feature of the *Pervigilium.*

[76] See section on the final stanza and the interpretation of the poem and Currie, 'Pervigilium Veneris', 220–4.

[77] D. Shanzer, 'Once Again Tiberianus and the Pervigilium Veneris', *Rivista di Filologia e di Istruzione Classica* 118, no. 1 (1990), 306–18.

metrical technique used in Tiberianus's *Amnis* has more differences than similarities with the *Pervigilium*. Just as with the arguments adduced in favour of Tiberianus, however, the evidence collected against him is not impermeable. Shanzer's rejection of Tiberianus turns on two key pieces of evidence,[78] firstly that the *Pervigilium* seems to have taken as a source for line twenty-six:

> Cras *ruborem, qui latebat veste* tectus *ignea*

lines eleven to twelve and sixteen to seventeen of the *Imminutio* of Ausonius's *Cento Nuptialis*:

> Perfidus alta petens ramum *qui veste latebat*
> Sanguineis ebuli bacis minioque *rubentem*
>
> . . .
>
> Est in secessu, tenuis quo semita ducit,
> *Ignea* rima micans: exhalat opaca mephetim.

Shanzer rightly highlights the striking verbal parallels: *qui latebat veste*, *ignea* and *rubentem/ruborem*. Ausonius composed his piece entirely out of sections of Vergil[79] – the highlighted words and phrases common to the *Cento Nuptialis* and the *Pervigilium* come from *Aeneid*, 6.406, *Eclogues*, 10.27 and *Aeneid*, 8.392 respectively. Shanzer argues that the author of the *Pervigilium* could not have been working directly from Vergil for his line twenty-six because only in Ausonius's work do all the key phrases and words appear together. For Shanzer, this means that the author of the *Pervigilium* must have

---

[78] G. B. Perini also rejects the arguments for Tiberianus's authorship. His 'Per la datazione del Pervigilium Veneris.' *Storia, letteratura e arte a Roma nel secondo secolo dopo Cristo. Atti del Convegno: Mantova 8–10 ottobre 1992* (1995), 139–58 takes on the arguments of both Cameron *and* Shanzer, and revives the interpretation of Schilling who proposed a second century date and saw in the *Pervigilium* a strong stoic flavour. Perini modifies this position slightly to avoid the arguments against a strong philosophical interpretation (the position of this edition) by proposing that the *Pervigilium*'s author was 'un stoico imperfetto'.

[79] Who, in fact, apologizes to the reader for using the Augustan poet to such explicit ends: *bis erubescamus, qui et Vergilium faciamus impudentem. Cento Nuptialis Parecbasis* to Chapter 7.

used Ausonius and accordingly that the poem must have been written after 368. This would put Tiberianus out of the picture.[80]

Shanzer's position on this point, however, appears tenuous on a number of grounds. Firstly, the author of the *Pervigilium* demonstrates extensive and unmediated knowledge of Vergil's *Georgics* (lines two, ten, and fifty-nine for example), *Eclogues* (line fifty-two) and most importantly *Aeneid* (lines sixteen, eighty-five and eighty-six) throughout the poem, so it is by no means impossible that he arrived at the image in line twenty-five independently of Ausonius. Secondly, leaving the phrase *qui latebat veste* aside (which must be Vergilian), the words *ignea* and *rubor* could happily have been arrived at by the author himself without any external influence because the words so perfectly fit the *Pervigilium's* poetic context. The word *ignea* refers to the *flammeum*,[81] the orange coloured Roman wedding veil, but at the same time, within the 'rose-maiden' metaphor of the third stanza, the fiery red of the rose petals covering the inner node of the flower.[82] Similarly the *rubor*,[83] both the inner deep red petals of the rose bud and the blushing modesty or, indeed, the sexual organs of the maiden, is the natural vocabulary choice for an author wishing to maintain his metaphorical imagery and 'double entendre' between the blossoming rose and blushing maiden which he has conjured in the stanza. Finally, the sheer contrast between the defloration described by Ausonius,[84] and the marked tenderness of the approach taken by the author of the *Pervigilium*,[85] prompts the question, why the author of the *Pervigilium* would make such a direct allusion, as Shanzer would have it, to this passage of Ausonius, so contradictory to the feeling and sentiment he is trying to cultivate in his own? It is, of course, possible that the

---

[80]   D. Shanzer, 'Once Again Tiberianus', 307–9.
[81]   See note on line twenty-five.
[82]   See note on line fourteen.
[83]   Again, I refer the reader to the note on line twenty-five.
[84]   This passage of Ausonius is so explicit that it is very rarely translated by editors.
[85]   Revealed in full in the note to line twenty-six.

author of the *Pervigilium* was aiming to profit from the technique of *Kontrastimitation*, if he did take this passage from Ausonius at all. It should be noted, however, that at this stage the argument comes down to subjective opinion since there exists, as far as I see, no further evidence to tip the case one way or another.

The second line of investigation along which Shanzer ventures for her rejection of Tiberianus is one of grammar. The argument centres on the prominent use of the preposition *de*, which Cameron discarded as a means of dating the text and takes as merely a metrical filler or idiosyncrasy.[86] I agree with Shanzer against Cameron in thinking that the poet's use of *de* can be taken as an important indication of his Latinity, but cannot be used to date the poem exactly. Shanzer attempts to show that the lack of this preposition, or other 'vulgarisms' in Tiberianus's other works, demonstrates that the *Pervigilium* cannot have been written by the same hand. However, Catlow identifies this feature of the *Pervigilium*'s style convincingly with that of the African writers Fulgentius and Augustine.[87] He cites Augustine's *Psalmus contra Partem Donati* – also written in trochaic tetrameter – where *de* appears twenty-eight times in 275 lines. This is without taking into account the refrain – another feature which the *Pervigilium* shares with Augustine's piece – which, if included, would bring the count up to one example of *de* in every four lines. Fulgentius shares the *Pervigilium*'s and Augustine's fondness for the preposition. Tiberianus held offices in Gaul, Spain and, most interestingly, Africa,[88] as part of his career and could well have been exposed to elements of more popular constructions while on duty. An explanation of his choice not to employ this register in his other four poems would be that the *Pervigilium* has an unmistakable 'air of folk-song',[89] which is evidenced

---

[86]   Cameron, *The Pervigilium Veneris*, 214–15.
[87]   Catlow, *Pervigilium Veneris*, 20, 56–7.
[88]   Duff and Duff, *Minor Latin Poets*, 555.
[89]   Catlow, *Pervigilium Veneris*, 57.

elsewhere by the choice of meter and use of rhyme and parallelism;[90] the use of *de,* in this case, is then another part of the poet's creation of a popular feeling set in contrast with the high literary artifice of the piece.[91]

A similar line of reasoning can be followed in response to Catlow's scepticism over Tiberianian authorship on the grounds of metrical differences between the *Pervigilium* and the *Amnis Ibat.*[92] Simply stated, cannot an author change his metrical style between pieces? That Tiberianus was a metrical experimenter can be shown by the widely varying meters of his surviving works, the *Amnis* in trochaic tetrameter catalectic, the poem on gold (2) and the *Hymn on the Supreme Being* (4) in hexameter, and the poem on the soaking bird (3) in hendecasyllables.

The limits of this argument are clear, but an early attempt to date the *Pervigilium,* first proposed almost 400 years ago, last considered in 1986 and left unexplored by scholarship since then, provides interesting evidence to suggest that the poem, if not written by Tiberianus himself, may at least have belonged to a similar time period and intellectual milieu.

Claude de Saumaise (Salmasius) (1588–1653) published his first edition of Solinus's *Polyhistor,* or *Collectanea rerum memorabilium* in 1629.[93] The work saw a second, improved edition in 1689.[94] Saumaise's edition represents a masterwork of scholarship. His edition of Solinus's heavily corrupt text takes up sixty-three pages in the second print and it is followed by no fewer than 943 pages of commentary, in two volumes, as well as by both an index of authors

---

[90] See Currie, 'Pervigilium Veneris', 215–20.
[91] See section on the final stanza and interpretation of the poem for the interpretation of this effect.
[92] Catlow, *Pervigilium Veneris,* 40–1.
[93] C. Saumaise, *Cl. Salmasii Plininae exercitationes in Caii Iulii Solini Polyhistora* (Paris: C. Morellus, 1629).
[94] C. Saumaise, *Cl. Salmasii Plininae exercitationes in Caii Iulii Solini Polyhistora*[2] (Utrecht: J. van de Water, J. Ribbius, F. Halma and G. van de Water, 1689).

cited and a general index. The introduction to the work considers what is known of Solinus's life, times and his relationship to various other classical authors. It also contains the text of what Saumaise calls the *Ponticon*, a fragment of twenty-two hexameter lines, ostensibly the beginning of an epic on the sea, which is attributed to Solinus in six of the manuscripts which preserve his *Polyhistor*.[95] Saumaise's edition of the *Polyhistor* remained authoritative – and widely read – until Theodor Mommsen's edition of 1895.[96] Mommsen, too, prints the *Pontica* at the end of his edition, but casts doubt over its attribution to Solinus.[97]

Saumaise, as we know, was also well acquainted with the *Pervigilium Veneris*. Manuscript S, Parisinus 10318 – the 'Salmasianus' – was given his name after he discovered it in 1615, and he proposed several emendations for difficult *loci* in the poem which have remained popular among editors to this day.[98] Saumaise's sensitivity to the language and idiosyncrasies of the authors he read and edited throughout his career as a textual critic led him to note certain parallels between the linguistic features of the *Pervigilium* and Solinus's *Polyhistor*. On page 194 of his commentary, for example, Saumaise makes the following assertion:

> Auctor Pervigilii Veneris, quem Catullum esse nullo iudicio volunt eruditi, cum sit mediae aetatis, et Solino supparis:
> [There follows a citation of the *Pervigilium*'s second stanza, lines nine to eleven.]

---

95   The *Ponticon, Pontica*, or *Halieuticon* as it has been variously named by later critics, was most recently edited by J. Blänsdorf, *Fragmenta Poetarum Latinorum Epicorum et Lyricorum*[4] (Berlin: De Gruyter, 2011) where it appears as number 76 among the *incertorum versus*. In his system of manuscript abbreviation, the Solnius MSS. A, B, C[1,2], E and M preserve the verses. Following Blänsdorf, I refer to the verses as the *Pontica* below.

96   T. Mommsen, *C. Iulii Solini Collectanea Rerum Memorabilium* (Berlin: Weidmann, 1895).

97   *Ibid.* 233–5.

98   See, *inter alia*, line sixty, where the *totis* of MSS STV is replaced by Saumaise's *totum*, or line eighty-one, where the Frenchman proposed *explicant* against *explicat* (STV).

Ita legendus ille locus. Fecit, id est, procreavit. Idiotismus illius aevi.[99]

He thus makes it clear that he believes Solinus and the *Pervigilium*'s author to belong to the same period on linguistic grounds. Saumaise returns to this point later in his commentary:

> Et *humorem* pro aqua posuit, ut paulo ante: *ipsumque fontem supero humore saginatum.* Et in Pervigilio Veneris:
> Tunc humore de superno, spumeo Pontus globo,
> Fecit undantem Dionem.[100]

And later, on the same word *(h)umor,* Saumaise comments:

> Expressit *maritum rorem* Solini, quum dixit permixtione roris margaritas concipi. Sic maritus imber apud autorem Pervigilii Veneris:
> Fecit undantem Dionem de maritis imbribus.[101]

He continues later in the same section of the commentary:

> Non dubium est quin rorem Solinus lunaris asperginis nomine designaverit.... Vetus poeta in Pervigilio:
> Humor ille, quem serinis astra sudant noctibus.
> Rorem intellegit. Veteris poetae fragmentum *rorifluam lunam* apellat:
> Quam nos rorifluam sectemur carmine lunam.
> Poema illud non rectiore iudicio tribuitur Varroni Atacino quam Pervigilium Veneris Catullo. Utriusque carminis auctor non longe fuit ab aetate Solini.[102]

The linguistic relationship that Saumaise proposes in these lines between Solinus and the *Pervigilium* was revisited in 1954 by

---

[99] Saumaise, *Plininae exercitationes in Caii Iulii Solini Polyhistora,* 196. For the false but, in the early modern period commonly accepted, attribution of the *Pervigilium* to Catullus, see n. 25 above.

[100] *Ibid.* 303. Note that Saumaise reads *humore* in line nine of the *Pervigilium* where in the present edition *cruore* is printed. This does not change Saumaise's point about the fact that Solinus, like the *Pervigilium* author, *humorem pro aqua posuit,* since *Umor* appears for water also in line twenty of the *Pervigilium.*

[101] *Ibid.* 796.

[102] *Ibid.* 796. The poem of the *vetus poeta* is number 483 in Riese, *Anthologia Latina,* fasc. 2: 1. The line cited by Saumaise is line fourteen in Riese's edition.

Gerardo H. Pagés at the University of Buenos Aires.[103] He returned to the topic in a second article in 1986.[104] In both pieces, Pagés refers to the linguistic characteristics which Saumaise highlighted in linking Solinus and the *Pervigilium*.[105] To this Pagés adds valuable evidence from the subject matter treated in both Solinus's *Polyhistor* and the *Pervigilium Veneris* to connect the two.[106] Solinus, for example, writes about the *Amyclae silentium* (*Polyhistor* 7.5), which appears in the *Pervigilium* in line 92.[107] He mentions the *favonii spiritus* (52.1), *Pervigilium* line fourteen, and makes the association between *rubor* and blood (30.34), *Pervigilium* twenty-two to twenty-six. To these and the other commonalities that Pagés finds, I would add the condensed history of Rome in the *Polyhistor* mentioning the key role of Romulus, born of Mars and Rhea Silvia (1.16–18) and the arrival of Aeneas along with his period of rule over the Latin lands (2.14–18), synthesized in the *Pervigilium* at lines sixty-nine to seventy-four, as well as the description of the plains of Sicily as *in floribus semper et omni vernus die* (5.14), *Pervigilium* fifty-two and fifty-three.

Pagés's articles also highlight the coincidences in material between the *Pervigilium* and Pliny's *Naturalis Historia* that are not mediated through Solinus, and include a detailed discussion of the attribution of the *Pervigilium* to a Florus of the second century, considered here above.[108] However, Pagés's most stimulating contribution to the date and authorship debate is the link he proposes between the *Pervigilium* and the *Pontica* attributed to Solinus. His evidence and arguments for

[103] G. H. Pagés, 'Rosas y Perlas en el *Pervigilium Veneris*', *Anales de Filología Clásica* 6 (1954), 197–205.
[104] G. H. Pagés, 'Sobre la datación del *Pervigilium Veneris*', *Anales de Filología Clásica* 11 (1986), 105–17.
[105] Pagés, 'Rosas y Perlas en el *Pervigilium Veneris*', 204–5; Pagés, 'Sobre la datación del *Pervigilium Veneris*', 115–16.
[106] Pagés, 'Sobre la datación del *Pervigilium Veneris*', 116.
[107] The following references to the *Polyhistor* follow the edition of Mommsen (1895).
[108] Pagés, 'Sobre la datación del *Pervigilium Veneris*', 115 and 106–14 respectively.

this association are collected in the earlier 1954 article 'Rosas y Perlas en el Pervigilium Veneris'. Pagés's proposal is unfortunately based on the unlikely identification of references to oysters and the production of pearls in both the *Pervigilium* and the *Pontica*:[109] while a reference to oysters in the *Pontica* is questionable, none at all appear in the *Pervigilium*'s line thirteen.[110]

If Pagés was misguided in relating the *Pervigilium* and the *Pontica* on the grounds of an illusory reference to pearls in the poems, there are nonetheless good grounds on which to see a connection between the two, which speak for the value of his reinvigoration of Saumaise's earlier observation. At a basic level, the vocabulary and images of the *Pontica* fragment and the stanzas of the *Pervigilium* which concern Venus's power, birth and fertility overlap to a considerable extent. Consider the *Pervigilium*'s second stanza alongside lines one to seven of the *Pontica*, for example, where *caerulas . . . catervas* (*Pervigilium* line ten) become *aequoreas . . . catervas* (*Pontica* line two), and the *spumeo . . . globo* (*Pervigilium,* nine) becomes *unda spumea* (Pontica, six). Compare, too, the *Pervigilium*'s line nine with lines four to seven of the *Pontica* in particular, where the birth process of Venus is described. Or the idea of Venus's universal power to inspire fertility and reproduction in the *Pervigilium*'s seventh stanza, lines fifty-nine to sixty-seven – in particular sixty-seven – and line seventy-seven (*Imbuit iussitque mundum nosse nascendi vias* (sixty-seven); *Rura*

---

[109] Pagés makes his claim for the references to pearls in 'Rosas y Perlas en el *Pervigilium Veneris*', 199: 'Pero, ¿por qué hemos de poner el acento sobre las rosas, escamoteando la referencia directa a las perlas, que apenas parecen servir de término de comparación?'

[110] While Pagés is clearly right in noting the shared mythological background of the *Pontica*'s opening lines and the *Pervigilium* (Pagés, 'Rosas y Perlas en el *Pervigilium Veneris*', 202), his reading of a reference to oysters and pearls in the two pieces is doubtful. For the *Pontica*, Pagés takes up the reading of N. E. Lemaire, *Poetae Latini Minores* (Paris: Lemaire, 1824). The *Pontica*, entitled *Ponticon* in Lemaire's edition, appears on p. 217. It is accompanied by a commentary in the footnotes. In the note to line three (*quaeque sub aestifluis Thetis umida continet antris*) Lemaire comments the following: *Hoc versu describit ostreas, quae aestu maris allatae in antris vel lacunis litoris resident*. This is a stretch at best. For the *Pervigilium*, Pagés's reference to pearls apparently lies in line thirteen's *gemmas*, which in the context cannot refer to anything but the flower buds as gems.

fecundat voluptas; rura Venerem sentiunt (seventy-seven)), with lines twelve to fifteen of the *Pontica*:

> Te fecunda sinu Tellus amplexa resedit
> ponderibus librata suis, elementaque iussa
> aethereas servare vices. Tu fetibus auges
> cuncta suis: totus pariter tibi parturit orbis.[111]

Indeed, aside from these verbal coincidences, the two poems have in common the underlying concept of Venus as the principal reproductive power of the world. In this they share two main models: the prayer to Venus at the opening of Lucretius's *De rerum natura* 1.1–49 as well as Vergil, *Aeneid* 6.724–32 and *Georgics* 2.325–33. For detailed notes on the *Pervigilium*'s use of these sources, as well as the striking verbal parallels between them and the poem's seventh stanza, I refer the reader to the commentary on lines fifty-nine to sixty-seven and lines seventy-six to seventy-nine below. In the *Pontica*, the conception of Venus's ability to inspire the creative forces of the universe is the same:

> Nam cum prima foret rebus natura creandis
> in foedus conexa suum, ne staret inerti
> machina mole vacans, tibi primum candidus aether
> astrigeram faciem nitido gemmavit Olympo.[112]

It reappears in lines twelve to thirteen and thirteen to fourteen (quoted above).

Moreover, within this context of the description of Venus's power, part of the common theoretical milieu of the Classical and Late Antique world (see note to line fifty-nine in the commentary to the text below), the *Pervigilium* and the *Pontica* share references to the

---

[111] *Pontica*, 12–15.
[112] *Pontica*, 8–11.

central passage in Vergil, *Aeneid* 6.724–32 from independent lines.

The *Pontica* contains a reference in its first two verses:

Tethya marmoreo fecundam pandere ponto
et salis aequoreas spirantis molle catervas

to *Aeneid* 6.729:

Et quae marmoreo fert monstra sub aequore pontus.[113]

While the *Pervigilium* references *Aeneid* 6.727 in its line sixty-two.[114]

The fact that the *Pontica* can be shown to draw on the same philosophical tradition as the *Pervigilium* leading back through Vergil to Lucretius brings us once again to the figure of Tiberianus, whose connections with the *Pervigilium* have already been discussed above. His *Hymn to the Supreme God* has been shown to contain numerous Lucretian references.[115] The most explicit of these have been confirmed, commented upon and set within the 'milieu culturale neoplatonico (ed ermetico, gnostico, pitagorico e "caldaico")' in which Tiberianus worked and composed his poetry.[116] It is precisely upon this generalized philosophical background that the *Pervigilium* author draws for the imagery of the poem's seventh stanza,[117] and, moreover, for the enigmatic 'twist' in the poem's final stanza.[118] The argument for a connection between the *Pervigilium* and the *Pontica* on the levels of both vocabulary and imagery has been made above. But previous scholarship has also seen an independent link between Tiberianus's *Hymn to the Supreme God* and the *Pontica*, once again through

---

[113] Vergil, *Aeneid* 6.729.
[114] See note to line sixty-two in the commentary below.
[115] T. Agozzino, 'Una preghiera gnostica pagana e lo stile lucreziano del IV secolo', *Dignam Dis a Giampaolo Vallot (1934–1966)*, ed. Istituto di Filologia latina dell'Università di Padova (Venice: Libreria Universitaria Editrice, 1972), 169–210, especially 95–201.
[116] F. Perono Cacciafoco, 'Sincretismo filosofico–religioso e tradizione nell'inno al *Deus Omnipotens* di Tiberiano', *Atene e Roma* (2nd new series) 4, no. 1–2 (2012), 90–110, citation on 99.
[117] Refer to commentary on lines fifty-nine to sixty-seven.
[118] See subchapter 'The Final Stanza and Interpretation of the Poem' below.

imitation of Lucretius, and the suggestion of a common intellectual milieu.[119] The strong interdependence between Tiberianus and the *Pontica* for which Agozzino argues is rightly treated cautiously by other scholars,[120] but it does not seem too much to suggest that the *Pervigilium*, the *Pontica* and the *Hymn to the Supreme God* belong to a common intellectual milieu, built on the same base of religious–philosophical stereotypes. They do not propound a specific, fixed doctrine, but rather draw on a common theoretical background.[121] The verbal similarities between the three pieces serve to anchor this suggestion to more stable evidence.

In the case of the *Pervigilium*, where the provenance, author, and date of the poem remain mysterious, Pagés's revival of Saumaise's old suggestion of a connection to the *Pontica* is valuable because it provides an extra point of reference from which to attempt to gather information about the poem. In revising and correcting Pagés's argument here, the important association he saw is now stronger. And in connecting this idea to the independent line of enquiry followed in recent years, which links the *Pontica* and Tiberianus's work, the context in which the *Pervigilium* was composed becomes, I believe, clearer.

---

[119] Perono Cacciafoco, 'Sincretismo filosofico–religioso', 104; Agozzino, 'Una preghiera gnostica pagana e lo stile lucreziano del IV secolo', 210; K. Smolak, *HLL* 5 (1989) §552.B: 266 ('Pervigilium Veneris', in *Handbuch der lateinischen Literatur der Antike*, ed. R. Herzog and P. Lebrecht Schmidt, 258–63 (Munich: C. H. Beck, 1989).

[120] Agozzino, 'Una preghiera gnostica pagana', 210. Hesitation over this strong claim can be found at Perono Cacciafoco, 'Sincretismo filosofico–religioso', 104–5.

[121] This idea is nicely expressed by Perono Cacciafoco at 'Sincretismo filosofico–religioso', 106.

The Meter

The *Pervigilium* is written in trochaic tetrameter catalectic, commonly called the trochaic septenarius on account of the missing syllable in its final foot. The first three metrons consist of a pair of trochees and the fourth of a trochee and a half:

$$-\cup \quad -\cup \; \vdots \; -\cup \quad -\cup \; \vdots \; -\cup \quad -\cup \; \vdots \; -\cup -$$

As with most meters in Latin poetry the trochaic tetrameter catalectic had two forms in use, one following the more formal Greek model and another 'Latin' counterpart – somewhat more loosely constructed – to which the name *septenarius* specifically applies.[122] An example of an author who used the more formal type would be Seneca in his *Phaedra* 1201–12, *Oedipus* 223–32, and *Medea* 740–51, while Plautus makes use of the freer variety in his *Rudens*. The meter has several licences, common to both the formal and freer versions, which give variety to the line. Firstly, the second trochee in the metron can have its second syllable (the anceps) lengthened, making that foot a spondee ($--$). This is the case in the refrain of the *Pervigilium*:

Crās ămēt quī ⋮ nūmqu(am) ⁀ămāvīt, ⋮ quīqu(e) ⁀ămāvīt ⋮ crās ămēt

Secondly, long syllables can be 'resolved' into two shorts in any foot. This makes then a tribrach ($\cup\cup\cup$) if it appears in the first foot of a metron or an anapaest ($\cup\cup-$) if it occurs in the second foot of a metron. Resolution only takes place in the first foot of

---

[122] D. S. Raven, *Latin Metre* (Faber and Faber: London, 1965) presents the meter alongside its counterpart on facing pages. The formal version is called A and the freer variety B. I will use this shorthand in the following discussion. More recently, S. Heikkinen, 'The Resurrection and Afterlife of an Archaic Metre: Bede, the Carolingians and the Trochaic Septenarius', *Classica et Mediaevalia* 65 (2016), 241–81 has given an overview of the history of the study of the meter with particular emphasis on its description in Bede's *De arte metrica*.

a metron in one instance in the *Pervigilium*, in the middle of line thirty-one:

⋮ pŏsŭĭt ārmă ⋮

only twice in the second foot of a metron, making anapaests in the sixth foot of line seventy-six:

⋮ rūră Vĕnĕrēm ⋮

and in the second foot of line twenty-three:

Fāctă Cўprĭdīs ⋮

Finally, the lengthened anceps from the first variation can also be resolved, which makes, in effect, a dactylic foot, as is the case in the sixth foot of line ten:

⋮ īntĕr ēt bĭpĕd ⋮ (ēs)[123]

And the second foot of line seventeen:

Ēn! Mĭ ⋮ cānt lăcrĭ ⋮ (mǣ)[124]

However, the *Pervigilium* also has some licences not permitted by the type A tetrameter and which are only found in the freer type B practice. These 'deviations' from the stricter model are few and their scarcity has caused some editors to attempt to emend them away.[125] More recent work on the poem has shown, however, that for the most part these divergences are part of normal Roman use of the trochaic tetrameter catalectic.[126] The *Pervigilium* can, then, be considered an example of the Roman trochaic septenarius, that is to say in the freer type B, but towards the stricter end of that group.

---

[123] (*ēs*) is included to show the entire word and bracketed only to show that it is not part of the sixth foot.
[124] (*mǣ*) is bracketed on this line for the reason stated in note 123.
[125] Notably Clementi, *Pervigilium Veneris, The Vigil of Venus*, 84.
[126] Catlow, *Pervigilium Veneris*, 36–42; Cameron, *The Pervigilium Veneris*, 218.

The exceptions to the type A model all involve the substitution of a spondee, or the spondee equivalent anapaest,[127] in the first foot of a metron, which in type A had to be kept as a pure trochee. The exceptions are as follows:

On line thirty-five a spondee (*inermis* STV) appears in the third foot;

On line fifty-one spondees (*praesens* STV, *adesederunt*) occur in the first and fifth feet respectively;

On lines sixty and ninety-one spondees (*vernis, nec me*) occur in the fifth foot;

On lines fifty-six and sixty-two anapaests (*pueri, aleret*) appear in the fifth foot.

In five out of the seven exceptions to the type A model the spondee or anapaest occurs in the fifth foot. The first foot spondee on line fifty-one (*praesens*) has been emended on grounds of meaning as well as for the reason that it would be the only first foot spondee in the entire ninety-three line poem were it left as found in the MSS.[128] Following this I have adopted the emendation of E. Courtney which similarly mends the sense of line thirty-five while removing another lone example of a spondee in the third foot of a line.[129] This leaves us with the conclusion that the author of the *Pervigilium* permitted spondaic or anapaestic fifth feet occasionally throughout his piece.[130]

The trochaic tetrameter catalectic was used with relative frequency in the dialogue of Greek tragedy and it was adopted by the Romans, although not put to great use in the Golden Age of Latin

---

[127] It is equivalent in that the long–short (−∪) trochee has its second syllable lengthened to become a long–long spondee (−−): the short–short–long (∪∪−) anapaest merely divides the first syllable into two shorts. Thus the foot is still equivalent to a spondee.

[128] See note on this line in the commentary.

[129] E. Courtney, 'Pervigilium Veneris 35', *The Classical Journal* 100, no. 4 (2005), 401–2.

[130] Looking back to the discussion of authorship and date, Tiberianus's *Amnis Ibat* also permits the occasional fifth foot spondee, doing so in lines six and fourteen.

literature.[131] It appears in the plays of Plautus and Terence where it is fitted, especially in Plautus, to the natural strong stress accent in Classical Latin on the penultimate syllable of words where that syllable is long or on the antepenultimate syllable if the penultimate syllable is short.[132] This evidently suits the trochee where, if a stress accent is used, the weight of the stress falls on the first syllable in the foot. Indeed, this was probably part of the reason that the meter was a favourite for soldiers' chants and marching songs:

> Caesar Gallis subegit, Nicomedes Caesarem;
> Ecce Caesar nunc triumphat qui subegit Galliam[133]

where, importantly, the accent and ictus always coincide.[134] The catalectic last foot is also well suited to a language in which a trisyllabic word with a short penultimate syllable will fit neatly inside the last metron. The meter was next picked up by Seneca,[135] who strove to meet the strictures of the Greek model, and by Florus, who is almost as strict in his usage.[136] Tiberianus, of course, uses the meter at the start of the fourth century in his secular *Amnis ibat*, but the trochaic tetrameter was also adopted and given an injection of energy by writers of early Christian hymns. Hilary of Poitiers in his *Hymnum dicat turba fratrum*, for example, exhibits a tetrameter which shows little regard for the strict form of the meter, while in contrast Prudentius's tetrameters are metrically very rigorous.[137]

---

[131] Raven, *Latin Metre*, 74.
[132] For Latin's strong stress see W. S. Allen, *Vox Latina* (Cambridge: Cambridge University Press, 1970), 86. For its position see L. R. Palmer, *The Latin Language* (London: Faber and Faber, 1954), 221.
[133] Suetonius, *Divus Iulius*, 49, cited by D. Norberg, *Introduction à l'étude de la versification médiévale* (Stockholm: Almqvist and Wiksell, 1958), 74.
[134] Norberg, *Introduction à l'étude de la versification médiévale*, 74.
[135] *Phaedra* 1201–12, *Oedipus* 223–32 and *Medea* 740–51.
[136] For Florus's claim to authorship of the *Pervigilium* see the above discussion of authorship.
[137] W. B. Sedgwick, 'The Trochaic Tetrameter and the "Versus Popularis" in Latin', *Greece and Rome* 1, no. 2 (1932), 96–106.

The trochaic tetrameter catalectic's diaeresis often occurs after the fourth foot of the line, as in the *Pervigilium*'s refrain:

Cras amet qui ⫶ numqu(am) ⌐amavit, ‖ quiqu(e) ⌐amavit ⫶ cras amet

The first half of the line is then sometimes split into two again at the end of the second foot. The poet of the *Pervigilium* uses this technique occasionally in conjunction with a repetitive line structure, for example in lines twenty-four and sixty-five:

Deque gemmis | deque flammis ‖ deque solis purporis
Perque caelum | perque terras ‖ perque pontum subditum

It might be considered that this line structure lends itself to this type of repetition when a similar pattern can be found at Plautus, *Pseudolus*, 695[138] for example:

Scis amorem | scis laborem ‖ scis egestatem meam

In the introduction to his edition of the poem Formicola has tabulated the various line patterns which the author of the *Pervigilium* has used in the piece.[139] Counting the refrain only once, the pattern with a trochee in the first foot of the metron and a spondee in the second is by far the most common, appearing thirty-eight times out of eighty-three lines. This is followed by varying arrangements of trochees in the first foot and trochees or spondees in the second. All together these usages account for seventy-two out of eighty-three lines. Add to this the formally permitted tribrachs and second-foot dactyls and anapaests and there are a total of seventy-seven lines within the bounds of the standard usage of the formal trochaic tetrameter catalectic. Only the five lines discussed above containing a fifth-foot spondee or its equivalent anapaest belong to the tradition of the tetrameter catalectic's more informal cousin, the trochaic

---

[138] Cited in Norberg, *Introduction à l'étude de la versification médiévale*, 74.
[139] Formicola, *Pervigilium Veneris*, 42.

septenarius. The metrical practice of the author then, who, in line with my conclusion above, on grounds of date, style, meter, and philosophical outlook, is most probably Tiberianus, can be situated at the more rigorous end of the septenarius tradition. To facilitate the reader's own comparison of the *Pervigilium* and Tiberianus's verse, style and tone, I have included as an appendix his two key works discussed above: the *Amnis ibat* and the *Omnipotens*.

The Final Stanza and Interpretation of the Poem

The concluding stanza of the *Pervigilium Veneris* is characterized by a return to the rural setting invoked in stanzas one, three, five, six, and nine. The bulls are stretched out with their partners, as are the sheep. The birds are singing. The poet draws the reader's attention to the *puella Terei*, the nightingale, and comments on the paradox of the beauty of her song and its tragic mythical origins.[140] But the poet then steps into the frame himself and directly addresses the audience. He poses the reader two questions and in the second he expresses his desire to become like the *chelidon*, the swallow:

Illa cantat, nos tacemus. Quando ver venit meum?
Quando fiam vel chelidon ut tacere desinam?

She sings, I am silent. When will my spring come?
When will I be like the swallow even, and break my silence?

The poet next explains the cause of his distressed appeal:

Perdidi musam tacendo, nec me Phoebus respicit.

I have lost my muse in staying silent and Phoebus is ignoring me.

He finishes his poem by comparing his own silence to that of the proverbially silent town of Amyclas,[141] and then by repeating the refrain one final time.[142]

Previous editors have concentrated on the very appropriate selection of the *Philomela–Procne* myth for the poem and in particular

---

[140] See note on line eighty-six.
[141] Adage *AC* 692 in Erasmus of Rotterdam's collection which is also the first known mention of the *Pervigilium* (*AC* 809). See also note on line ninety-two.
[142] E. K. Rand, 'Spirit and Plan of the Pervigilium Veneris', *Transactions and Proceedings of the American Philological Association* 65 (1934a), 1–12 calls this final repetition of the refrain 'a masterstroke of irony'.

the poet's longing to become like the swallow which, while still in human form, had its tongue cut out to prevent exposure of Tereus's crime, and which, upon transforming into a bird, regained its speech.[143] Commentators have been seduced by the appearance of the nightingale, whose beautiful yet melancholy song has enjoyed great symbolism in the Western literary tradition,[144] and do not consider the role of the swallow at all.[145] Of the three birds in the *Philomela–Procne* myth, only the swallow is specifically named and it is the only one with which the author of the *Pervigilium* associates himself directly.[146] In view of this fact it is my belief that the significance of the bird in the final stanza and in the poem in general deserves more attention than it has previously been given and that it offers new insight into the interpretation of the poem.

In the first place, the swallow has been celebrated as the herald of spring in literature since at least Aristotle's *Nicomachean Ethics*:

μία γὰρ χελιδὼν ἔαρ οὐ ποιεῖ . . .[147]

For one swallow does not make a summer . . .

The suitability of the poet's association with the swallow in the context of the final stanza and in the poem at large, which celebrates the spring festival of Venus, is evident.[148] However, even in Aristotle's reference to the swallow as the harbinger of spring, the ambiguity of the sign is apparent. The first swallow of the year does not bring the

---

[143] See for example Catlow, *Pervigilium Veneris*, 97 and Schilling, *La Veillée de Vénus*, 29.

[144] A. R. Chandler, 1934, 'The Nightingale in Greek and Latin Poetry', *The Classical Journal* 30 (2), 78–84. See also Coleridge's *The Nightingale* and Keats's *Ode to a Nightingale* for example.

[145] See for example Rand, 'Spirit and Plan of the Pervigilium Veneris', 11 and Clementi, *Pervigilium Veneris, The Vigil of Venus*, 259–61.

[146] The poet uses the Greek *chelidon* for the Latin *hirundo*. This is one among the various Graecisms used throughout the work, see note on line seven for example.

[147] Bekker 1098a. The phrase features in Erasmus's *Adagia* latinized as *una hirundo non facit ver* (*AC* 692) and is often quoted in English in the somewhat archaic form 'one swallow doth not a summer make'.

[148] *Quando ver venit meum?*

warmer months straightaway but proclaims the start of the transitional and unsettling period which will yield to summer.

The ambiguity of the season of spring has been immortalized in T. S. Eliot's description of April in the opening lines of *The Waste Land* as 'the cruellest month', but the *topos* was present even in Classical literature. In Ovid's *Tristia* 3.12, spring is evoked with the traditional images:

> Frigora iam Zephyri minuunt . . .
> prataque pubescunt variorum flore colorum

> The winds of Zephyrus are lessening the cold . . .
> And the fields are blossoming with flowers of various shades,

the swallow makes her appearance at line nine.[149] However, in concordance with the mixed feelings that spring evokes, Ovid's poem finishes with a reflection on his exile in Tomis and the sadness he feels at being sentenced to make his home there.

The three spring odes of Horace *Solvitur acris hiems* (1.4), *Diffugere Nives* (4.7) and *Iam veris comites* (4.12) also involve a shift from the images of spring to darker considerations.[150] In the first, Horace switches suddenly from the celebration of spring to a deliberation on the fact that death comes to all. In the second spring poem a similar change of tone occurs from images of the dancing nymphs and Graces – who also appear in the *Pervigilium* at lines fifty-one, and fifty-four to fifty-five – to characters of myth locked in the underworld. The final vernal poem of Horace does the very same thing. The earth is free from the bonds of winter:

---

[149] Interestingly the swallow denies her connection with the *Philomela–Procne* myth: *malae matris crimen deponat hirundo*, just as the nightingale seems to do in the *Pervigilium* at lines eighty-seven and eighty-eight.

[150] The poems are analysed in the account of spring in Latin lyrics in J. J. Wilhelm, *The Cruelest Month: Spring, Nature and Love in Classical and Medieval Lyrics* (New Haven: Yale University Press, 1965), 4–5.

iam nec prata rigent nec fluvii strepunt
hiberna nive turgidi.

The fields are no longer stiff nor are the rivers rushing
From their swelling with the winter snow.

But in the next stanza the *Philomela–Procne* myth rears its head and changes the tone of the poem:

nidum ponit, Ityn flebiliter gemens,
infelix avis et Cecropiae domus
aeternum opprobrium, quod male barbaras
regum est ulta libidines.

The unhappy bird makes her nest
Bewailing tearfully her Itys and the eternal disgrace
Of the Cecropean house, because she wickedly avenged
The barbarous[151] lusts of kings.

Horace finishes by advising his friend, a certain Vergil, to set aside business and, bearing in mind death (*ignes nigri*),

Misce stultitiam consiliis brevem
Dulce est desipere in loco.

Mix a bit of tomfoolery with your prudence
It's good to play around on occasion.

It is clear from these examples from the Classical authors that the contemplation of spring leads the mind to consider not just the seasonal changes that will bring warmer temperatures and life, but also the passing of time and ambiguity of change. It is also a time when the joys of life abounding are liable to be set in contrast with any lack of joy in an individual's life. The inherent potential melancholy of

---

[151] Compare *Pervigilium* line eighty-eight where Tereus is referred to as *maritus barbarus*.

spring, as well as the ambiguity of the swallow as a symbol of the changing seasons, form the backdrop for the poet's distressed appeal in the final stanza of the *Pervigilium*. The ambiguity of the swallow brings further significance to the interpretation of the poem in a number of other ways. The swallow's call was not known to be particularly melodious. Indeed, anyone listening to the call of the most ubiquitous European swallow (*hirundo rustica*) will immediately understand why it was associated with talkativeness, chattering or a foreign tongue in Latin:

Garrula (quam) tignis nidum suspendat hirundo.

The chattering swallow builds her nest in the rafters.[152]

But most importantly for the *Pervigilium* – which uses the Greek word for swallow – the swallow's voice is strange and barbarous in the Greek tradition,[153] as well as being associated with talkativeness:

τῶν χελιδόνων δόξειεν εἶναι λαλίστερος

He might appear to be more talkative than the swallows.[154]

The poet of the *Pervigilium Veneris* underlines the lowliness of the swallow's call by placing it in contrast with the tuneful song of the nightingale, which he describes in line eighty-seven as speaking with an *os musicum*. Such emphasis on the swallow's humble call in comparison with that of the nightingale is significant for the interpretation of the final stanza because it is with the *swallow* that the poet associates himself. In the spirit of the *Pervigilium*, the key line bears repeating:

---

[152] Vergil, *Georgics* 9.307.
[153] Klytemnestra speaking to the chorus about Kassandra. Aeschylus, *Agamemnon* 1050–2.
[154] Theophrastus, *Characters*, Λαλία.7.

Quando fiam vel chelidon ut tacere desinam?[155]

When will I be like the swallow even, and break my silence?

The poet only wants to be like the swallow; he does not think highly enough of his song to compare it with that of the nightingale. Indeed, he would be happy just to have back the ability to sing even if it is just with the voice of the chattering swallow.

The poem at large demonstrates the conflicted and ambiguous feeling of the poet towards his own song in several ways: he has chosen to write a highly literary poem in a meter often associated in antiquity with popular genres and sub-literary chants.[156] Indeed, some commentators have gone as far as calling it 'the meter *par excellence* of doggerel and jingles'.[157] The conflict between the highly allusive and artificial style of the poem and the meter chosen as its medium has already been noted,[158] and even when the increasing popularity of the meter for more serious literary works in the late antique and early mediaeval periods is taken into consideration, a certain disconnect remains in the case of the *Pervigilium*. The meter was taken up by Christian writers such as Prudentius and Hilary of Poitiers and became an important meter of early Christian hymnography, yet although the *Pervigilium* is closest to the usage of these authors,[159] it contains no hint of Christian thought or imagery. It is a markedly classical poem. This leaves the *Pervigilium* in a no-man's land: from a Classical point of view the meter is an odd fit with the literary aspects

---

[155] For the reading of *vel* for the MSS *ut* see note on line ninety.

[156] Sedgwick 'The Trochaic Tetrameter and the 'Versus Popularis' in Latin', 96–106; Norberg, *Introduction à l'étude de la versification médiévale*, 74; E. Fraenkel, 'Die Vorgeschichte des versus quadratus', *Hermes* 62, no. 3 (1927), 361.

[157] Cameron, *The Pervigilium Veneris*, 216.

[158] Cameron, *The Pervigilium Veneris*, 217: 'Nothing in Latin or for that matter Greek poetry before *c.* 300 explains why the author of the PV thought the trochaic septenarius appropriate for his poem.'

[159] Cameron, *The Pervigilium Veneris*, 217; see also Norberg, *Introduction à l'étude de la versification médiévale*, 74–5 for the peculiarities of these authors' use of the meter.

of the poem and in the period when the meter became popular for more serious literary endeavours, the *Pervigilium*'s strong classical themes and allusions do not fit with its Christian milieu.

Another aspect of the poem which signals the ambiguity of the poet's song and, perhaps, his own insecurity about it, is the mixture of poetic successes in the poem with sections and lines which are somewhat less worthy of praise. The memorable 'rose-virgin' stanza stands out in the poem as a triumph of metaphor. Our poet suggests the connection between flower and maiden throughout the stanza; the *surgentes papillae* of line fourteen, the play on the *pudor* (nineteen) and *rubor* (twenty-five) which is so suggestive that one editor indeed conjectured that the first be read in place of the second[160] and the *umens peplum* of line twenty-one are some examples of this delicate development of the corresponding images before the poet realizes the comparison towards the end of the stanza in line twenty-two:

Ipsa iussit mane totae virgines nubant rosae.

She herself ordered all the virgins to wed in the morning as roses.

Note also within this stanza how the poet skilfully manipulates the spectator's gaze on lines seventeen to nineteen,[161] and the vivid explosion of colour in between lines twenty-three to twenty-five.[162] It almost goes without saying that the 'last lovely flower of ancient verse'[163] must be considered to have accomplished something worthwhile to receive the praise and attention that it has done since its discovery at the turn of the sixteenth century.[164] However, critics have noted weak sections of the poem such as the prosaic line

---

[160] For Baehrens's *pudorem* for *ruborem* line 25, see the apparatus criticus on this line.

[161] See the notes to these lines in the commentary.

[162] 'Il s'abandonne à une sorte de variation chromatique ... On dirait l'esquisse d'une symphonie en rouge majeur.' Schilling, *La Veillée de Vénus*, lv.

[163] F. J. E. Raby, *A History of Secular Latin Poetry in the Middle Ages*, 2 vols, vol. 2 (Oxford: Clarendon Press, 1957), 46.

[164] See the subchapter below on the reception of the poem from the sixteenth century onwards.

thirty-eight,[165] and the 'flat' lines of stanza eight which 'quite lack the evocative power of the poem as a whole'.[166] This is to say nothing of the treatment of the final reference to the silence of Amyclae which is '[neither] logically or artistically relevant'[167] to the poem and was even left out of the translation of J. W. Duff for *The Literary History of Rome in the Silver Age*. It was presumably felt to be an anti-climax after the intriguing and passionate personal plea from the author in the previous lines which gives the poem its unique flavour.

The poet's familiar vocabulary and syntax gives the poem a popular feel. These familiar features include, notably, the usage of the preposition *de* where more standard Latin usage would prefer a variety of different constructions, which so offended some of the more puristic early editors of the poem,[168] as well as the use of the *praesens pro futuro*, a common feature of vulgar Latin.[169] But this is in contrast to the literary allusiveness of the poem, which shows that the author was well acquainted with a wide range of the best classical authors including Vergil, Ovid, Propertius and Horace and frequently referred to them in his poem. He adopted Vergilian phrases, *bipedes equi* (line ten) and *balantum grex* (line eighty-three) among various others, and even entire images such as lines fifty-nine to sixty-three, for example.

The paradox that the poet presents to the reader in the final stanza forms the final part of the poem's ambiguity and the poet's conflict. The poet claims to be silent: *nos tacemus; tacere desinam?; perdidi musam tacendo*, but he has just sung one of the most memorable and celebrated poems of late antiquity.

The direct connection that the poet draws between himself and the swallow, whose song is considered second rate to that of its sister the

---

[165] Formicola, *Pervigilium Veneris*, 139.
[166] Catlow, *Pervigilium Veneris*, 86.
[167] P. Pascal, 'The Conclusion of the Pervigilium Veneris', *Neophilologus* 49 (1965), 3.
[168] See note on line four.
[169] Rollo, 'The Date and Authorship of the Pervigilium Veneris', 406–7. See also the note for example at line seven.

nightingale – and which is an uncertain sign of a season which is itself ambiguous – reveals to the reader the distress with which the poet is suffering in the final stanza. Indeed, he informs us of the source of his troubles himself:

Perdidi musam tacendo, nec me Phoebus respicit.

The poet's internal conflict – perhaps insecurity – about his own song can be observed throughout the body of the poem in the choice of meter, the blend of traditional elevated language with more popular and common turns of phrase, and the shifts from occasional poetic brilliance to sections of dubious merit. This poetic tension is summed up by the assertion which the poet makes – while singing – that he has lost his song.

The poet nowhere in the poem makes mention of a lover, or lack thereof. Nevertheless, it is hard, given the theme of the poem in general, not to connect the poet's anguished plea in the final stanza to matters of love in some way, especially when the final repetition of the refrain serves to ironically underline the dumb predicament of the poet, a refrain which has been rightly said to imply 'an awareness of a universal desire for love existing outside the limits of the self'.[170] It is important to note that the refrain demonstrates this universality of love rather than a personal outlook; the final stanza contains none of the indications that the poet is writing himself as an *exclusus amator*, and the consideration of Venus as the goddess of love throughout the poem is literally universal, covering all aspects of her role from the creative force of the universe (stanza seven) to her guardianship of a girl's maturation into womanhood (stanza two). Nor can the *musa* of line ninety-one be said with any certainty to represent a lost lover. While Ovid's Sappho in *Heroides* 15 connects the loss of a lover to a loss of song,

---

[170] Wilhelm, *The Cruelest Month*, 19.

Efficite ut redeat: vates quoque vestra redibit,
Ingenio vires ille dat, ille rapit[171]

Make him come back: for he will also bring back your poetic powers,
He gives power to your skill but he also takes it away

the muse in the classical tradition more powerfully represents divine inspiration and signals that the author is operating within a poetic genre.[172] The popular modern meaning of a muse as a lover who directly inspires the creative process, often towards love poetry, does not exist in this tradition explicitly.

However, to come back to Ovid's association of love and song in the *Heroides*, a couplet in the *Anthologia Latina*, which is remarkable in its similarity to the refrain of the *Pervigilium* in respect of both its use of parallelism and its universal appeal to love, connects the two directly:

Cantica gignit amor et amorem cantica gignunt.
Cantandum est ut ametur et ut cantetur amandum[173]

Love gives birth to song and song to love.
To be loved one must sing and to be sung one must love.

It is not, therefore, unreasonable to think of the cause of our poet's silence as stemming from some trouble in affairs of love. The poet does not, however, say this himself. The connection occurs in the mind of the audience thanks to the 'love-ly' context in which the poet's appeal is heard.

This mental connection is closer to the changes of mood and switch to the first person that characterize some mediaeval lyrics

---

[171] *Ibid.* 205–6.
[172] The famous muse invocations demonstrate this: Homer, *Odyssey* 1.1; Vergil, *Aeneid* 1.8–11; Hesiod, *Theogony* 1–35; Horace, *Carmina* 1.24.1–4.
[173] *AL* 271, ascribed to Tuccianus and demonstrating, notably, much of the parallelism and repetition of phrases inverted which has been observed in the *Pervigilium* by Currie, 'Pervigilium Veneris', 216–20 and n. 31.

rather than the more logical, even if not immediately obvious, progression from the invocation of spring to the reflection on the inevitability of death in Horace's *Diffugere nives*[174] for example.[175] In addition to Pascal's example from the *Carmina Cantabrigiensia*, the same unannounced leap to the first person from a third person contemplation of a spring setting can be found in the *Carmina Burana* in poems 85 and 146 among other examples.[176] Poem 85 (*Veris dulcis in tempore*) begins by introducing Iuliana who is sitting beneath the typically verdant spring bower. The poet introduces his own voice in the fourth and final stanza – if he had the girl he desired he would kiss her joyfully underneath the leaves – the implication, of course, is that he does not have his dream girl. The first stanza of poem 146 (*Tellus flore*) paints the spring scene with images reminiscent of those found in the *Pervigilium*:

Tellus flore vario vestitur
Et veris presentia sentitur,
Philomela dulciter modulans
Auditur; sic hiems sevitia finitur.

The earth is clad with variegated flowers
And spring's presence is felt,
Philomela's sweet song is heard,
So winter's cruelty is ended.

The poet goes on to describe the romantic subject of his poem with blushing cheeks and her hair loose. At the end of the fourth and penultimate stanza the poet makes his cry for help:

---

[174] *Carmina*, 4.7.
[175] P. Pascal, 'The Conclusion of the Pervigilium Veneris', 4, taking the Cambridge song *Verna Feminae Suspiria* as an example of a poem where the link between the initial image conjured by the poet and the closing abstract expression of emotion in the first person is supplied entirely in the mind of the reader.
[176] Compare for example poems 143 and 153.

Subvenias, mi domina, cadenti!

Help me my mistress, I am falling!

He continues his appeal in the last stanza and reveals what sudden emotional sensation has brought on his sadness:

Vulneratus nequeo sanari,
Nulla vite poterit spes dari, nisi
Me pre ceteris velis consolari,
Que cuncta vincis forma singulari.

I am wounded and unable to be cured,
No hope of life will be forthcoming, unless
You wish to console me before all others,
You who surpass everyone in your singular beauty.

Regardless of the technique or the nature of the poet's distress, the crucial feature of these poems – including the *Pervigilium* – is the feeling of the 'sudden stab of irrational apprehension in the midst of pleasure or happiness' that they describe.[177] Indeed, this is nothing new to study of the *Pervigilium* and precisely the reason why the opening line of Eliot's *The Waste Land* is quoted so ubiquitously in discussions of spring and the mixed feelings it brings,[178] but the implications of this poetic trope for the *Pervigilium* perhaps need to be revisited.

Currie noted that the Neo-platonic idea that full engagement in an activity, observing and recounting the joyous transformations of spring in the case of the *Pervigilium*, Horace, *Carmina* 1.4; 4.7 and 4.12 and the Wordsworth quoted in the footnote below for example, is

---

[177] Currie, 'Pervigilium Veneris', 222

[178] Also Wordsworth's *Intimations of Immortality from Recollections of Early Childhood* stanza 3: 'Now, while the birds thus sing a joyous song,/And while the young lambs bound/As to the tabor's sound,/To me alone there came a thought of grief . . .' distils this feeling very precisely (cited in Currie, 'Pervigilium Veneris').

only possible when one is not self-consciously aware that one is carrying out the activity:

Οὐ γὰρ τὸν ἀναγινώσκοντα ἀνάγκη παρακολουθεῖν ὅτι ἀναγινώσκει καὶ τότε μάλιστα, ὅτε μετὰ τοῦ συντόνου ἀναγινώσκοι· οὐδὲ ὁ ἀνδριζόμενος ὅτι ἀνδρίζεται καὶ κατὰ τὴν ἀνδρίαν ἐνεργεῖ ὅσῳ ἐνεργεῖ· καὶ ἄλλα μυρία· ὥστε τὰς παρακολουθήσεις κινδυνεύειν ἀμυδροτέρας αὐτὰς τὰς ἐνεργείας αἷς παρακολουθοῦσι ποιεῖν.[179]

When one reads, one is not necessarily aware that one is reading especially if one is paying particular attention when reading. Nor does someone acting bravely think about the fact that he is acting bravely while doing it, and there are myriad other examples. So conscious awareness enfeebles those very actions of which one becomes conscious.

This lends precision and clarity to an interpretation of the *Pervigilium* which was criticized by Catlow as 'a compound of carelessness ... and pervasive superficiality dressed up in critical jargon.'[180] However, on the interpretation of the final stanza and its implication for the poem as a whole, I believe that Wilhelm is right. He suggests that the poet painted a picture of a festival for Venus, the springtime, and love as a universal principle so alluring that he was himself drawn into it. I would further this view, in light of the evidence collected above to show the poet's internal conflict and self-consciousness over his poem, by proposing that the very self-consciousness the poet brings into his own picture triggers his faltering and realization of the humbleness of his song. The mannered way in which the poet introduces his personality into the poem perhaps points away from a strictly biographical reading of the twist in the final stanza, but the dearth of external information on the poem coupled with the very intimate nature of the appeal in the first person certainly invites a biographical reading of the poem's author or, more correctly, his poetic persona.

---

[179] Plotinus, *Enneads* 1.4.10.
[180] Catlow, *Pervigilium Veneris*, 98 gives his opinion of Wilhelm, *The Cruelest Month*.

The Literary Reception of the *Pervigilium* 1578–*c.* 1800

Soon after Pierre Pithou published the *editio princeps* of the poem in 1578, awareness of the *Pervigilium*, along with its fame, naturally began to increase. The piece was not just popular among scholars, whose numerous critical editions attest to a vibrant interest in the poem in the centuries after its discovery.[181] A number of literary works also reveal a lively engagement with the *Pervigilium* at the same time. Despite this impressive *fortuna*, studies of the *Pervigilium*'s literary reception have been comparatively small.[182] This overview will also be small, but hopes to shed light on a particularly understudied group of literary responses to the poem.

I have chosen to deal with the reception history of the poem from the late-sixteenth century to the early-nineteenth for two reasons: at the earlier end, while the mediaeval poems of the *Carmina Cantabrigensia* and the *Carmina Burana* mentioned above, for example, might appear to contain vague echoes of the *Pervigilium*, untangling the general literary commonplaces about love, spring and the natural world – frequently to be found in almost all ages of Latin literature – from direct reception of the *Pervigilium* is an enormous and always uncertain task. After the first reliable reference to the poem by Erasmus

---

[181] After Pithou's first edition, there followed in quick succession an edition by Justus Lipsius in 1580, by Janus Dousa the Younger in 1592 (*Coniectanea in Catullum, Tibullum, Propertium* (Leiden Officina Plantiniana, apud Franciscum Raphelengium, 1588), by Petrus Schriverius in 1638, 'Animadvertiones in Pervigilium Veneris', in *Dominici Baudii Amores*, ed. Petrus Schriverius, 437–68 (Leiden: Hegerus and Hackius, 1638), and by physician and botanist Augustus Rivinus in 1644 (*Anonymi sed antiqui tamen poetae elegans et floridum carmen de vere, communiter Pervigilium Veneris inscriptum* (Leipzig and Frankfurt am Main: J. Pressius, 1644). After a pause of over 100 years, editorial interest in the piece picked up again at the end of the eighteenth century with the edition of Wernsdorf in 1782. For the full list of editions of the *Pervigilium* see A. Cucchiarelli, *La veglia di Venere. Pervigilium Veneris: Introduzione, traduzione e note* (Milan: Biblioteca Universale Rizzoli, 2003), 61–3.

[182] Schilling dedicates two pages (xii–xiii) of his history of the text to the reception of the poem particularly in French literature, for example. Cucchiarelli also includes a short two-page section on the *Pervigilium*'s reception (48–9), and Smolak offers perhaps the most detailed summary of the poem's *fortuna* in one page (263) of his *HLL* entry.

and, more significantly, its *editio princeps,* this task becomes much less problematic because it is certain that the *Pervigilium* was known to scholars by this time. The reason for choosing the later date for ending this short overview of the *Pervigilium*'s reception history is simply that the poem's reception after 1809 is (relatively) well known. After the appearance of a version of the poem's refrain in Chateaubriand's *Les Martyrs* in 1810, the *Pervigilium* later played a central role in the narrative of Walter Pater's *Marius the Epicurean* (1885) and, perhaps most famously, in 1922 the first part of line ninety (there printed as *quando fiam uti chelidon*) found its way into T. S. Eliot's *The Waste Land.* These are celebrated authors and their reception of the *Pervigilium* has previously been studied.[183] The group of authors I want to consider now is much less well known outside specialist circles and their texts are only rarely mentioned in connection with the *Pervigilium.* While some of the texts presented here are clearly related to one another – they either come from the same literary circle or represent imitations of one another – it is difficult to trace a clear hereditary line in the reception history. For this reason, I will simply follow a chronological arrangement in what comes below.

Ten years after Pithou's small edition – the pamphlet comprised just four pages – and seven years after the text's appearance in Justus Lipsius's more readily available *Electorum Liber I* in 1580,[184] French Neo-Latin poet and senior official in the French court of Henry III, Jean Bonnefons (Joannes Bonefonius, 1554–1614), published a *Pervigilium Veneris* as part of his collection entitled *Pancharis* in 1587.[185] On the surface, Bonnefons's *Pervigilium* does not appear to

---

[183] For the *Pervigilium* in *Marius the Epicurean* see D. Romano, 'La genesi ed il significato del *Pervigilium Veneris* nella interpretazione di Walter Pater', *Annali del Liceo classico G. Garibaldi di Palermo* 11–13 (1974–76), 289–95. A. Booth dedicates a chapter to the *Pervigilium* in *The Waste Land* in her monograph *Reading The Waste Land from the Bottom Up* (Basingstoke: Palgrave Macmillan, 2015), 237–42.

[184] Published in Antwerp. The *Pervigilium* appears on pp. 35–46.

[185] J. Bonefonius, *Pancharis* (Paris: Ex officina Abelis l'Angelier, 1587), 30–5.

share much with the original apart from the title: at 147 verses it is longer than its late antique model. Moreover, Bonnefons uses Catullus's hendecasyllable for his poem, doing away with the original's characteristic trochaic verses. Nor does he opt for a refrain, another feature which distinguishes the earlier poem and which would later become, alongside the final stanza, one of its best known elements. Indeed, even at a deeper level Bonnefons does not seem to have relied very heavily on the *Pervigilium Veneris* for his inspiration either. What was, in the original, ostensibly a hymn to Venus praising her various mythological aspects on the night of her festival in Sicily, has now become in Bonnefons's text a song in celebration of a night of love-making. Only certain verbal and conceptual similarities in the context of the poem's title allow us to call Bonnefons's piece the first example of the *Pervigilium*'s reception after its rediscovery.[186] Bonnefons seems to have had in mind the *Pervigilium*'s third stanza for the vocabulary in lines twenty-one to twenty-nine emphasized in the passage below, for example,

> At te per faculas tuas *micantes*
> et haec aemula *purpurae* labella
> Oro perque genas et hunc capillum,
> Qui formosa vagus flagellat ora,
> Oro perque sinus et has *papillas*
> Primulum tibi iam sororiantes.
> Has *gemmas* geminas pari decore
> *Surgentes geminis* pares pyropis,
>
> ...

---

[186] That Bonnefons's poem is the first evidence of reception of the *Pervigilium* is the justified claim of W. Ludwig's article 'Giovanni Pontano und das *Pervigilium Veneris* das Jean Bonnefons', *Neulateinisches Jahrbuch* 4 (2002), 197–213. Aside from a text of Bonnefons's poem and a German prose translation, Ludwig's article also advances the convincing thesis – as the title suggests – that Bonnefons's *Pervigilium Veneris* owes more to Giovanni Pontano's *Hendecasyllaborum Libri II* (the *Baiae*) than it does to the *Pervigilium* for much of its imagery and inspiration.

Note also the repetition of *perque*, perhaps echoing the *Pervigilium*'s line sixty-five. For his lines sixty-eight to seventy-one, to take just one more example, the Neo-Latin poet borrows the image of Venus's power spreading throughout the body from the *Pervigilium* lines sixty-three to sixty-four:

Dum strictim appliciti arctore vinclo
Haeremus calidi, *Venusque venis*
Diffusa interioribus, tepente
Artus languidulos liquore rorat,

. . .

In this passage, too, the words *tepente* and *rorat* echo the *Pervigilium*'s second stanza, where Bonnefons would have read Lipsius's *tepentes* for *patentes* in line fifteen.

Bonnefons's *Pancharis*, and his *Pervigilium Veneris* with it, became popular at the end of the sixteenth century and into the seventeenth and eighteenth centuries as well.[187] Perhaps most effective for its circulation among the Latinate literary circles of the period was the poem's appearance in the first volume of Janus Gruter's popular and widespread *Delitiae Poetarum Gallorum* in 1609.[188] Moreover, in 1588, the year after Bonnefons's *Pervigilium* first appeared, a version was also made available to a French-reading public in the *Imitations* of Bonnefons's friend Gilles Durant (1554–*c*. 1614).[189] Indeed, Durant's imitation was frequently printed alongside Bonnefons's original in the years after its publication. The French version follows the structure and narrative of the Latin closely but does not remain so close to the original text that it can be called merely a translation. Durant's rhyming couplets and fondness for

---

[187] For the publication history of the *Pancharis* see Ludwig, 'Giovanni Pontano und das *Pervigilium Veneris*', 197–98 (nn. 4–6). For the reception of Bonnefons's *Pervigilium* in England particularly, see below in this chapter.

[188] J. Gruter [Rhanutius Gherus], *Delitiae Poetarum Gallorum*, 6 vols (Frankfurt am Main: J. Rosa, 1609). Bonnefons's *Pervigilium Veneris* is in vol. 1, pp. 679–83.

[189] G. Durant, *Imitations tirées du Latin de Jean Bonnefons, avec autres amours et meslanges poétiques, de l'invention de l'Autheur* (Paris: L'Angelier, 1588).

repeated structures (he repeats the formula 'tant de ...' seventeen times in the last twenty lines of the poem) make for a more charming but less forceful effect in the imitation than in Bonnefons's Latin.

While the works of Bonnefons and Durant experienced a wide circulation in the decades following their publication, the next piece of evidence for the *Pervigilium*'s early modern reception remained almost completely unknown until January 1975, when the British Library acquired the manuscript now numbered Additional MS. 58435. This item is the manuscript notebook of Robert Sidney (1563–1626), Earl of Leicester, brother of Sir Philip Sidney and father of Lady Mary Wroth (to whom we will come shortly). It contains a collection of sonnets, songs, pastorals and epigrams, which Robert probably composed in the late 1590s.[190] The notebook was an exciting find for the study of Elizabethan poetry, stemming as it does from the important literary environment of Penshurst. The collection is also an exciting testimony of the *Pervigilium*'s reception in English literature, since its *Song 3* (item 7 in the sequence) is a counter-imitation, or parody, of the *Pervigilium*.[191] Sidney may have seen the poem in Lipsius's Antwerp edition of 1580, for example, during his time in Flushing (Vlissingen) in the southwest Netherlands, where he was made Governor in 1588 and where he would stay for the next fifteen years.[192]

The song's refrain makes its parodic character clear right from the outset:

Loue not whoe haue not lou'd
and whoe doe loue, loue no more

---

[190] P. J. Croft, in the edition of the manuscript *The Poems of Robert Sidney. Edited from the Poet's Autograph Notebook* (Oxford: Clarendon Press, 1984), remains necessarily cautious about the poems' dates of composition and the time at which they were revised and written up as a fair copy in the notebook (p. xiv and n. 2).

[191] Song 3 appears on pp. 148–55 of the Oxford edition.

[192] A short biography of Robert Sidney in the context of the manuscript is given in H. Kelliher and K. Duncan-Jones, 'A Manuscript of Poems by Robert Sidney: Some Early Impressions', *The British Library Journal* 1, no. 2 (1975), 107–8.

Aside from the obvious verbal parallelism in the refrain, Sidney also signalled his reference to the *Pervigilium* in the lines' formal aspects too: in contrast to the iambic tetrameter employed throughout the verses of *Song 3*, the refrain has a trochaic rhythm as revealed in its second line. Likewise, the refrain's couplet is the only unrhymed verse in the whole collection, perhaps intended to suggest the lack of rhyme in the original Latin chorus.[193]

The counter-imitation of the *Pervigilium* in Sidney's refrain is sustained throughout *Song 3*, where winter imagery symbolizes the situation of the abandoned lover. Indeed, the first word of Sidney's poem after the refrain is 'Winter', in direct opposition to the *Ver* of the original. But to characterize *Song 3* as simply a parody of the *Pervigilium* would be to miss Sidney's sensitive response to the final stanza of the Latin piece in his own final verses:

Thus sayd a shepheard, once
wth weights of change opprest
For hee had lost at once
what euer hee lou'd best
And saw whyle hee did mourn
the worlds fayre looks renewed
whyle hee a state past rewed
w[ch] neuer would retourn.

These lines read like a poetic commentary on the *Pervigilium*'s verses eighty-nine to ninety-two: in Sidney's reading the *Pervigilium* poet becomes a shepherd (perhaps in reponse to the bucolic imagery of the final stanza) whose unhappiness, exacerbated by the changing seasons (wth weights of change opprest), at losing something he cares deeply about (*perdidi musam tacendo* – the ambiguity of the Latin *musa* is expressed in Sidney's 'whatever') sets him in contrast with the positive

---

[193] These points are made by Croft in the Introduction to the Oxford edition (p. 32).

changes in nature he sees around him (the worlds fayre looks renewed). This makes him doubtful that his previous joy will ever return (*quando ver venit meum?*/ wch neuer would retourn).

Given the intensity of literary activity around Penshurst, it comes as no surprise to find another echo of the *Pervigilium* in the work of another member of the Sidney family, this time from Robert's daughter Mary. Her *Song 1*, the seventh poem in the autograph Folger manuscript probably written in 1610, begins with the line 'The spring now come att last'.[194] It is a variation on Robert Sidney's *Song 3*, as evidenced, for example, by the echo of Robert's lines sixty-three and sixty-four:

> This said a shepherd, once
> With weights of change oppressed,

in lines seventeen and eighteen of Wroth's version:

> A shepherdess thus said
> Who was with grief oppressed

Aside from this reference to her father's interpretation of the *Pervigilium* and the repositioning of the poem's temporal timeframe in spring, Wroth's *Song 1* shows little engagement with the Latin original, if any at all. Overall, *Song 1* belongs much more to the tradition of vernacular pastoral poetry. As Paul Salzman observes in his note on the poem in the La Trobe online edition of Wroth's poetry: 'As a pastoral song ... it relates to the immense popularity of pastoral in the sixteenth and seventeenth centuries, manifested especially, in relation to Wroth, in Philip Sidney's work, especially within Arcadia.'[195]

---

[194] P. Salzman *et al.*, *Mary Wroth's Poetry: An Electronic Edition* (2012). Available online: http://wroth.latrobe.edu.au/index.html (last accessed 7 June 2017). The edition's 'Textual Introduction' gives the likely date of composition of the Folger manuscript as 1610.

[195] Salzman, *Mary Wroth's Poetry* (last accessed 7 June 2017).

If Wroth's *Song 1* contains only a reverberated echo of the *Pervigilium*, with the next piece we return to more direct reception of the late antique piece. Jacob Balde (1604–1668) was one of seventeenth-century Germany's most important Neo-Latin poets. A four-volume collection of his poems appeared within Balde's own lifetime,[196] and an *opera omnia* edition was produced in 1729 in eight volumes.[197] Among this impressive output is the *Philomela* (first published 1645), a collection of poems totalling over 1600 verses and composed in a wide variety of meters, in which the song of the nightingale is converted into a Christian song for the love of God. Balde's *Philomela* is an innovative paraphrase of the *Philomena* of the English theologian and Archibishop of Canterbury, John Peckham (1230–1292). In line with the contemporary *communis opinio*, Balde believed the *Philomena* to have been written by Saint Bonaventure (1221–1274) as he makes clear in the title of his work: *Paraphrasis lyrica in Philomelam D. Bonaventurae doctoris Ecclesiae.*[198]

One of the final poems of the *Philomela* is the *Epinicium divini Amoris animam triumphatam ad coelestem sponsum subvehentis.* Its refrain immediately indicates the poem's relationship to the *Pervigilium*:

Nunc amet quae non amavit, quaeque amavit nunc amet![199]

---

[196] J. Balde, *Poemata,* 4 vols, vol. 4 (Cologne: Busaeus, 1660).

[197] J. Balde, *Jacobi Baldi Opera poetica Omnia,* ed. M. Happach and F. X. Schlütter, 8 vols, vol. 8 (Munich: Typis Joannis Lucae Straubii, 1729). This edition was reprinted with introduction in 1990: *Jacob Balde SJ: Opera poetica omnia.* Neudruck der Ausgabe München 1729, ed. with introduction W. Kühlmann and H. Wiegand, 8 vols, vol. 8 (Frankfurt am Main: Keip, 1990).

[198] For the word games behind the titles *Philomena* and *Philomela,* see Thill's article: A. Thill, 'La *Philomela* de Jacobus Balde. Création poétique dans une paraphrase néolatine', *Revue des études latines* 58 (1980), 428–48 (pp. 432–3). Thill deals with the reception of the *Pervigilium* in Balde's *Philomela* more specifically on pp. 438–40.

[199] The refrain is repeated eight times throughout the *Epinicium* and divides eight, equally long stanzas of six lines each. For the text of the *Epinicium* in what follows, I use the 1729 *Opera Omnia* edition of Balde's works: Jacobus Balde, *Philomela* in Happach and Schlütter (eds.), *Opera poetica Omnia*: 249–50. For a discussion of the meaning of Balde's version of the refrain, see Schilling's article on the *Epinicium*: R. Schilling, 'Une résurgence chrétienne du "Pervigilium Veneris" au 17ème siècle: l'Epinicium divini Amoris de Jacob Balde', in *Balde und Horaz,* ed. E. Lefèvre, K. Haß and R. Hartkamp (Tübingen: Gunter Narr Verlag, 1999), 375–9.

Balde employs the *Pervigilium*'s trochaic tetrameter throughout the piece and suggests the language and style of the late antique original in a number of the *Epinicium*'s lines.[200] But the scheme of Balde's poem differs significantly from that of the late antique *Pervigilium*. The first two stanzas describe the passion of the soul which has been struck by divine love (*Mens anhela cordis aestu sic dolet iucundius*, line eight). The next two stanzas treat the celebration of the soul's arrival in heaven (*Una vox est: Gaudeamus, una vox, sed plurium*, line twenty-four), while the final four stanzas describe the figurative wedding of the soul with Christ (*Sponsa, dormi: tendit, ecce, Sponsus ipse bracchia*, line forty). Despite these obvious differences in tone and theme between the two pieces, however, commentators have identified two underlying ideas which bind the *Pervigilium* and the *Epinicium* and which, perhaps, encouraged Balde to adopt the *Pervigilium* as a model for this piece: the first relates to the figure of Philomela herself: while the *Pervigilium*'s Philomela (the nightingale) is the sorrowful young wife of Tereus in line eighty-six, in Balde's *Philomela* the nightingale becomes the voice of the Christian soul in the *Epinicium* – she undergoes a positive transformation in Balde's Christianized version.[201] Secondly, the *Pervigilium* poet presents his piece as a song for the festival of Venus – as a ritual song – though the final stanza confirms that it is a literary imitation of ceremonial poetry. In the same way, Balde creates a literary version of the mystical epithalamium, a tradition which goes back to the Bible's *Song of Songs*.[202]

– After Balde and in the second half of the seventeenth century continuing well into the eighteenth, poetic translations of the *Pervigilium*

---

[200] There's the echo of the *Pervigilium*'s repetition in Balde's lines six (*per . . . per . . .*) and eleven (*nec . . . nec . . .*), for example.

[201] Thill, 'La *Philomela* de Jacobus Balde', 439.

[202] Schilling, 'Une résurgence chrétienne du "Pervigilium Veneris"', 379; Thill, 'La *Philomela* de Jacobus Balde', 440.

became increasingly common, beginning with the *Venus' Vigils* of Thomas Stanley (1625–1678) in 1649.[203] As intended translations, and thus not entirely original literary creations, the relationship of these works to the original text is less complex than the instances of reception considered above. Accordingly, I will mention just a selection of these texts as representative of the group: in France there was *La traduction d'une himne sur les Fêtes de Vénus* by Noël-Étienne Sanadon (1676–1733) in 1728,[204] which was followed by a *Traduction en prose et en vers d'une ancienne hymne sur les fêtes de Vénus* by an anonymous author offering the rather wordy translation of the refrain:

> Jeunes coeurs, à l'amour hâtez-vous de rendre:
> Demain tout reconnoit ses droits.
> Et vous, qu'amour jadis rendit sensible et tendre,
> Aimez demain comme autrefois.[205]

Back in Britain, and just before Sanadon's 1728 version, 'Graveyard poet' Thomas Parnell (1679–1718) published a translation of the *Pervigilium*, included in his *Poems on Several Occasions* in 1721.[206] Parnell's rendering of the refrain is perhaps one of the best in English:

> Let those love now, who never lov'd before,
> Let those who always lov'd, now love the more.

The same year saw a curious episode in the *Pervigilium*'s reception history with the publication of *The Pleasures of Coition; or, the nightly*

203 T. Stanley, *Europa. Cupid crucified. Venus' Vigils. With annotations, by Tho. Stanley Esq.* (London: Printed by W.W. for Humphrey Moseley, 1649).

204 N.-É. Sanadon, *La traduction d'une himne sur les Fêtes de Vénus avec des remarques critiques sur la même pièce* (Paris: de la Roche, 1728).

205 *Traduction en prose et en vers d'une ancienne hymne sur les fêtes de Vénus, intitulée Pervigilium Veneris* (London and Paris: Barbou, 1766). The author leaves only the initials L. D. P. for posterity.

206 Thomas Parnell, *Poems on several occasions: Written by Dr. Thomas Parnell, ... and published by Mr. Pope*, ed. A. Pope (London: printed for B. Lintot, 1721), 47–67. The translation was printed with a Latin text of the *Pervigilium* alongside it.

sports of Venus: a poem. The anonymous piece, as its extended title declares, is a translation of Jean Bonnefons's *Pervigilium* of 1587.[207] *The Pleasures of Coition* renders Bonnefons's Latin faithfully for the most part, but occasionally translates the already unambiguous imagery of the original even more explicitly:

> At first I hand in hand engag'd;
> Then at distance threw a dart;
> Last a full push I made, enrag'd
>   Which pleasing, pierc'd her vital part,
> Each answers ev'ry stroke, their part each play,
> We boldly act, and all love's duties bravely pay.

(157–63)

Later in the eighteenth century and now in Germany, Gottfried August Bürger (1747–1794) also produced at least three poetic translations of the *Pervigilium* which represented for him a high point of 'classical' literature expressed in popular meter. Believing, as frequently in the early modern period, the *Pervigilium* to have been written by Catullus, the poem provided a model for Bürger's own poetic aims to treat high themes in a popular style.[208] Indeed, Bürger wrote an essay offering a detailed analysis of the *Pervigilium* in relation to his own poetics, which was published posthumously in 1802.[209] Bürger's first attempt at rendering the *Pervigilium*'s refrain, first published in 1773 in the *Teutsche Merkur*,[210]

---

[207] *The pleasures of coition; or, the nightly sports of Venus: a poem. Being a translation of the Pervigilium Veneris, of the celebrated Bonefonius. With some other pieces* (London: for E. Curll at the Dial and Bible, 1721).

[208] L. L. Albertson, 'Pervigilium Veneris und Nachtfeier der Venus. G. A. Bürgers Liedstil und sein lateinisches Vorbild', *Arcadia - Internationale Zeitschrift für Literaturwissenschaft*, 16, no. 1–3 (2009), 1–12.

[209] G. A. Bürger, 'Rechenschaft über die Veränderungen in der Nacht feier der Venus', in: *Gottfried August Bürgers sämtliche Schriften*, ed. K. Reinhard, 4 vols, vol. 4 (Göttingen: H. Dieterich, 1796–1802), 471–596.

[210] *Teutsche Merkur*, April 1773, pp. 20–30. The publication history of the *Nachtfeier* is given in P. Kahl (ed.), *Das Bundesbuch des Göttinger Hains: Edition - historische Untersuchung - Kommentar* (Tübingen: Walter de Gruyter, 2006), 336–7.

Morgen liebe, wer die Liebe
Schon gekannt!
Morgen liebe, wer die Liebe
Nie empfand!

is more straightforward than the third version that appeared in his
Sämtliche Schriften in 1796:

Morgen liebe, was bis heute
Nie der Liebe sich gefreut!
Was sich stets der Liebe freute
Liebe morgen, wie bis heut![211]

With the last item in this overview, we come to perhaps the most
intriguing example of the *Pervigilium*'s early modern reception: in
1772, Welsh philologist Sir William Jones (1746–1794) published an
anonymous volume entitled *Poems consisting chiefly of translations
from the Asiatick languages*.[212] The collection contains a poem called *A
Turkish Ode of Mesihi*, which is accompanied by a transliteration of
the original as well as a prose translation.[213] In the preface to the
volume, Jones includes a paragraph on the *Turkish Ode* in which he
draws attention to the similarities between Mesihi's poem and the
Pervigilium:

It is not unlike the *Vigil of Venus*, which has been ascribed to Catullus;
the measure of it is nearly the same with that of the Latin poem; and it
has, like that, a lively burden at the end of every stanza.[214]

---

[211] Bürger, *Sämtliche Schriften*, vol. 1, pp. 3–16.

[212] [W. Jones], *Poems consisting chiefly of translations from the Asiatick languages: To which
are added two essays, I. On the poetry of the Eastern nations. II. On the arts, commonly
called imitative* (Oxford: Clarendon Press, 1772).

[213] [Jones], *Poems consisting chiefly of translations from the Asiatick languages*, 103–13.

[214] *Ibid.* p. vi. Prishtinali Mesihi's (*ca.* 1470–1512) *Murabba'-i bahâr* (Ode to Spring) was
popularized in Europe chiefly through Jones's translation. On Mesihi and his reception
in Jones see R. Elsie, 'The Hybrid Soil of the Balkans: A Topography of Albanian
Literature', in *History of the Literary Cultures of East-Central Europe: Junctures and
Disjunctures in the 19th and 20th centuries*, ed. M. Cornis-Pope and J. Neubauer, 4 vols,
vol. 2 (Amsterdam, Philadelphia: John Benjamins Publishing, 2006), 283–301 (286).

There then came, in 1774, a Latin prose translation of Mesihi's poem in Jones's *Poeseos Asiaticae* – alongside the Turkish original in Arabic script – after which was printed a poetic Latin version of the *Turkish Ode*, entitled the *Carmen Turcicum*.[215] By way of explanation, Jones writes: *Poematis illius, quod* Veneris Pervigilium, *nominatur, haud est absimile; placuit igitur versionem poeticam numeris trochaicis contextam addere*.[216] The *Carmen Turcicum* appeared with both the English *Turkish Ode*, Mesihi's original transcribed in Roman letters and a prose translation of the original in the second edition of Jones's (still anonymous) *Poems consisting chiefly of translations* in 1777.[217]

It is easy to see why Jones felt inspired to compose a poem which responds to both Mesihi's *Murabba'-i bahâr* and the *Pervigilium*: apart from the similar subject matter and meter that Jones himself mentions, the poems both have memorable refrains. Jones translates Mesihi's refrain to English prose as, 'Be cheerful, be full of mirth; for the Spring soon passes away: it will not last.'[218] In his *Pervigilium*-inspired Latin poem, this becomes:

Nunc amandum est, nunc bibendum; floreum ver fugit, abit.

The poems also share numerous images central to their themes: to take a most striking example from the first stanza of the poems, Mesihi writes (again, in Jones's prose translation), 'Thou hearest the tale of the nightingale, "that vernal season approaches"'. In the *Carmen Turcicum*:

Alites audis loquaces per nemora, per arbutos,
Veris adventum canentes tinnulo modulamine.

215 W. Jones, *Poeseos Asiaticae commentariorum libri sex: cum appendice; subjicitur Limon, seu miscellaneorum liber* (London: T. Cadell, 1774), 222–9.
216 Jones, *Poeseos Asiaticae*, 222.
217 [W. Jones], *Poems consisting chiefly of translations from the Asiatick languages: To which are added two essays, I. On the poetry of the Eastern nations. II. On the arts, commonly called imitative* (London: N. Conant, 1777). The *Carmen Turicicum* is printed on pp. 94–6.
218 Jones's poetic version runs: 'Be gay, too soon the flowers of Spring will fade.'

Then there are the images of the dewdrops on spring flowers (Mesihi stanza six; *Carmen Turcicum* stanza four; *Pervigilium* stanza three); the comparison of virgins to roses (Mesihi stanza five; *Carmen Turcicum* stanza five, *Pervigilium* stanza three); the image of the year turning 'red' (Mesihi stanza six; *Carmen Turcicum* stanza seven; *Pervigilium* stanza three); or the internal reflection on the end of life prompted by the return of Spring (Mesihi stanza two; *Carmen Turcicum* stanza two; *Pervigilium* stanza ten) – the list could go on. Indeed, it would be fascinating to know if Mesihi's fifteenth- or sixteenth-century poem was in some way itself inspired by the *Pervigilium*, such are the number of parallels between the pieces. This must remain, however, the work of a specialist in Ottoman literature.

With so much in common in terms of theme and content between Mesihi, the *Pervigilium* and the *Carmen Turcicum*, it is no surpise to find in Jones's *Carmen* a large number of verbal resonances with its Latin model. These are similar to, but more explicit than, those we saw in Balde's *Epinicium*: we find, for example, the repeated tricolon structures of the *Pervigilium* in line twenty-seven:

Perque saxa, perque colles, perque lucos emicat.[219]

Or the use of *Ecce!* to indicate the start of a new development in the poem's imagery (*Carmen Turcicum*, lines five, thirteen and twenty-nine). Overall, Jones's forty-four-line blend of two earlier models, from two very different backgrounds, manages to steer a successful course between the dangers of over-imitation and culture-clash. And despite belonging to the latest pieces of reception of the *Pervigilium* in this survey, it must surely be among the most interesting.

---

[219] A tricolon with *quique* appears on line 6, for example.

Critical Text and Translation

Sigla

S   Codex Salmasianus Parisinus 10318, *saec.* VIII
T   Codex Thuaneus Parisinus 8071, *saec.* IX
V   Codex Vindobonensis 9401 (Sannazarianus), *saec.* XVI
   (1501–3)

Cras amet qui numquam amavit quique amavit cras amet!

Ver novum, ver iam canorum, vere natus orbis est;
Vere concordant amores, vere nubunt alites,
Et nemus comam resolvit de maritis imbribus.
Cras amorum copulatrix inter umbras arborum   5
Implicat casas virentes de flagello myrteo.
Cras Dione iura dicit fulta sublimi throno.

Cras amet qui numquam amavit quique amavit cras amet!

Tum cruore de superno spumeo Pontus globo
Caerulas inter catervas, inter et bipedes equos   10
Fecit undantem Dionem de maritis imbribus.

Cras amet qui numquam amavit quique amavit cras amet!

Ipsa gemmis purpurantem pingit annum floridis,
Ipsa surgentes papillas de Favoni spiritu
Urget in nodos patentes; ipsa roris lucidi,   15
Noctis aura quem relinquit, spargit umentes aquas.
En! Micant lacrimae trementes de caduco pondere;
Gutta praeceps orbe parvo sustinet casus suos.

---

1 amavit[1]] amabit S | amavit cras] cras amavit T || **2** vere] ver T | natus] natus STV: renactus *Baehrens*: laetus *coniecit. Riese*: renatus *Lipsius* orbis] iovis S: est iovis *Buecheler* || **3** amores] a maiores T | nubunt] nubent T || **4** comam resolvit] conam resolvet T || **5** amorum] amorem T || **6** casas] gaza S: gazas TV: casas *Pithou* || **7** fulta sublimi] fultas sublime S | throno] trono ST || **9** Tum] tunc SV: tuno T: tum *Cazzaniga* | cruore] quiuore T | superno] superbo S: superhuc T | globo] glovo T || **10** et bipedes] etui pedes T || **11** Dionem] Dione TV de ... imbribus] *delevit Buecheler* | maritis] maritis STV: marinis *Rivinus* | imbribus] fluctibus *Sanadon* || **13** gemmis] gemmas T floridis] floribus STV: floridis *Rigler* || **14** surgentes] turgentes *Scaliger* | Favoni] Faboni ST | spiritu] sparitu (y *supra* a) T: spyritu (u *supra* y) V || **15** Urget] urguet TV | nodos] notos S: totos TV: nodos *amicus Scriverii* | patentes] penates SV: pentes T: tepentes *Lipsius*: tumentes *Crusius*: feraces *Riese*: patentes *Wernsdorf*: tenaces *Formicola* || **16** relinquit] relinquid T | umentes] tumentis ST || **17** En Micant] et micanat S: et mecanat TV: emicant *Ach. Statius*: en micant *Schulzius*: et micant *Lipsius* | lacrimae] lacrimas S | caduco] cadum TV || **18** orbe] urbe S | sustinet] sustine S: sustenet V ||

Tomorrow let him love who never has before, and let he who has loved
  also love tomorrow!

Spring is new, spring is now full of song, in spring the world was born.
In spring lovers come together, in spring the birds wed,
And the wood lets down her hair under nuptial downpours.
Tomorrow, in the shade of trees, the lovers' matchmaker   5
Weaves verdant bowers out of myrtle shoots.
Tomorrow Dione rules enthroned on high.

Tomorrow let him love who has never before, and let he who has loved
  also love tomorrow!

Then out of celestial blood in a frothy ball,
Amidst the sea-blue shoals and his two-footed horses,   10
Pontus made the flowing Dione out of fertile rains.

Tomorrow let him love who never has before, and let he who has loved
  also love tomorrow!

It is she who paints the purpling year with flowery gems,
She who encourages the swelling buds with the West Wind's breath
Into their unfolding nodes; she who sprinkles the moistening waters   15
Of glittering dew that the night breeze leaves behind.
Look! The trembling teardrops glitter with their unsteady weight;
And the dripping bead in a small sphere checks its fall.

En! pudorem florulentae prodiderunt purpurae.
Umor ille, quem serenis astra rorant noctibus,   20
Mane virgineas papillas solvit umenti peplo.
Ipsa iussit mane totae virgines nubant rosae;
Facta Cypridis de cruore deque Amoris osculis
Deque gemmis deque flammis deque solis purpuris
Cras ruborem, qui latebat veste tectus ignea,   25
Unico marita nodo non pudebit solvere.

Cras amet qui numquam amavit quique amavit cras amet!

Ipsa nymphas diva luco iussit ire myrteo;
It puer comes puellis, nec tamen credi potest
Esse Amorem feriatum, si sagittas vexerit.   30
Ite nymphae, posuit arma, feriatus est Amor;
Iussus est inermis ire, nudus ire iussus est,
Neu quid arcu, neu sagitta, neu quid igne laederet.
Sed tamen nymphae cavete quod Cupido pulcher est:
Totus est armatus idem quando nudus est Amor.   35

Cras amet qui numquam amavit quique amavit cras amet!

'Conpari Venus pudore mittit ad te virgines,
Una res est quam rogamus: cede virgo Delia,

---

19 En] in STV: en *Bouhier* | pudorem] pudore | florulentae] rorulentae *coniecit Cazzaniga*: florulentae STV || **20** noctibus] notibus T || **21** virgineas] virgines V | papillas] papilla T | solvit] solvi T | umenti] tumenti ST || **22** Ipsa iussit] ipiussit T | mane totae] manet tute S: mane tuae T: mane tute V: mane ut udae *Ach. Statius*: mane totae *Orelli*: mane nudae *Mackail*: mane tutae *Scaliger* || **23** Facta] facta S: fusta T: fusta *supra* furta V | Cypridis] prius STV: Cypridis *Buecheler*: Paphies *Clementi*: patrio *Cazzaniga*: proles *Formicola* | osculis] S *et Sannazarius* osculis: oculis TV **25** ruborem] pudorem *Baehrens* || **26** Unico] unica ST: unica *supra* -at V: unico *Pithou*: uvido *Wernsdorf* | marita] marito T | nodo] noto S: loco TV: *Sannazaius* luco | iussit] lusit V || **29** It] et STV: It *Pithou* | comes] comis TV || **30** vexerit] exuit *Baehrens* || **31** Ite] in te S || **32** nudus] nudos S: durus T || **33** Neu] ne *coniecit Baehrens* | arcu neu] acuneo T | igne] digne T || **35** Totus ... armatus] est in armis totus *Saumaise et Schrijver metri causa* | armatus] inermis STV: in armis *Pithou*: armatus *Courtney* || **36** Cras ... amet²] *post 36 lacunam indicaverunt Riese et Catlow* || **37** Conpari] conparis *Baehrens*: non pari *Ussani* | ad te] ante *Baehrens* || **38** Una] unam S | res] re T | cede] caede V ||

Look! The purple blossoms have uncovered their blush!
That dew, which the stars let fall as dew on clear nights, 20
Will release the virginal buds from their sodden cloaks at daybreak.
She herself has ordered all the virgins to wed in the morning as roses;
The rose, made from the blood of the Cyprian, from Love's kisses
From jewels and flames and the purple glow of the sun,
Will not be ashamed to reveal her crimson tomorrow, which lay hidden
and 25
Protected beneath a robe of flame, as a bride, from a single knot.

*Tomorrow let him love who never has before, and let him who has loved
also love tomorrow!*

The goddess has ordered the nymphs to go to the myrtle grove.
The boy Cupid goes along as the companion of the girls, but Love
cannot be believed
To be at leisure if he has brought along his arrows. 30
Go nymphs, he has surrendered his arms, Love is on holiday;
He has been commanded to go unarmed, he has been commanded to
go naked,
So that neither with his bow, nor with his arrows, nor with his torch
might he do harm.
However, nymphs beware, for Cupid is handsome:
Love is fully armed even when he is naked. 35

*Tomorrow let him love who never has before, and let him who has loved
also love tomorrow!*

'Venus has sent us maidens to you equal in virtue,
We ask but one thing: leave, virgin Delia,

Ut nemus sit incruentum de ferinis stragibus
Et rigentibus virentes ducat umbras floribus.   40
Ipsa vellet te rogare si pudicam flecteret;
Ipsa vellet ut venires si deceret virginem.
Iam tribus choros videres feriatis noctibus
Congreges inter catervas ire per saltus tuos,
Floreas inter coronas, myrteas inter casas.   45
Nec Ceres, nec Bacchus absunt nec poetarum deus.
Detinenda tota nox est, pervigilanda canticis.
Regnet in silvis Dione, tu recede Delia!'

Cras amet qui numquam amavit quique amavit cras amet!

Iussit Hyblaeis tribunal stare diva floribus;   50
Praeses ipsa iura dicit, adsederunt Gratiae.
Hybla totos funde flores, quidquid annus adtulit,
Hybla florum sume vestem quantus Aetnae campus est!
Ruris hic erunt puellae vel puellae montium,
Quaeque silvas quaeque lucos quaeque fontes incolunt;   55
Iussit omnes adsidere pueri mater alitis,
Iussit et nudo puellas nil Amori credere.

---

39 Ut ... sit] utne nussit T | nemus] venus V: S *et Sannazarius* nemus | incruentum]
incruendum T | stragibus] tragibus S || **40** rigentibus] rigentibus STV: recentibus
Scaliger: vigentibus *Sannazarius* | virentes] vergentes T: virgentes V: virentes *Sannazarius*
| ducat umbras] duoad umbra S || **41** Ipsa ... flecteret] *versum omisit* T | vellet] vellit S |
te rogare] erogare SV: te rogare *Saumaise* || **42** vellet] vellit S | deceret] diceret T || **43**
choros] chorus S | feriatis] feriatos *Pithou* || **45** myrteas] myrteo S: mysteas T || **46**
Bacchus] baccas T | poetarum] potearum S | deus] deas T || **47** Detinenda] detinente S:
detinent et TV: detinenda *Heinsius*: continenter *Cazzaniga*: quod decenter *Formicola*: te
sinente *Prasch* | pervigilanda] perviclanda S: pervigila T: pervigil a V || **50** Hyblaeis]
hybei S: ybleis T || **51** Praeses] presens ST: praesens V: praeses *Scaliger* | dicit adsederunt]
dicet adsidebunt *Dousa* || **52** totos] totus S | funde] fundet S | flores] *omisit* S | annus]
annos S: annis T: annus *Sannazarius* || **53** sume vestem] superestem S: rumpereste T:
rumpe vestem V: sume vestem *Heinsius*: subde messem *Schriverius* quantus] quant T |
Aetnae] etnec S: ethne T: Ennae *Lipsius* || **54** montium] montium STV: fontium
Sannazarius et Baehrens || **55** quaeque¹] quae S: -que T | lucos] locus S: locos T | fontes]
montes STV: fontes *Schriverius* || **56** pueri ... alitis] mater alitis dei *Buecheler* alitis] alitis
S *et Sannazarius*: alitas TV || **57** et] at *Baehrens* | nudo] nullo T | Amori] amoti T |
credere] cedere *Schmitz* ||

So that the woods may be unstained by the slaughter of wild animals
And it may draw out its luxuriant shadows over untrampled flowers.   40
She would have been willing to ask you if she might bend your virtue:
She would have liked to ask you to come if it were fitting for a virgin.
You would now have seen, for three nights of festival,
Chorus bands moving along your paths amongst gathered groups
Amongst wreathed flowers and amongst the myrtle bowers.   45
Neither Ceres, nor Bacchus, nor the god of poets is absent.
The whole night should be extended and kept vigil with song.
May Dione reign in the woods! You, Delia, leave!'

Tomorrow let him love who never has before, and let he who has loved
   also love tomorrow!

The goddess has ordered her court to be decked with Hyblean
   flowers,   50
She presides and exercises jurisdiction, the Graces have sat down
   around.
Hybla, pour out all your flowers, whatever the year has brought!
Hybla, don your flowery cloak, as far as the plain of Aetna extends!
The girls from the countryside will be here, even the girls from the
   mountains,
As well as those who dwell in the woods and the groves and the
   fountains;   55
The winged boy's mother commands them all to take a seat around
And she instructs the girls to have no faith in naked Love.

Cras amet qui numquam amavit quique amavit cras amet!

Cras erit quo primus Aether copulavit nuptias
Ut pater totum crearet vernis annum nubibus,　　　　　　　　60
In sinum maritus imber fluxit almae coniugis

Unde foetus mixtus omnis aleret magno corpore.
Ipsa venas atque mentem permeanti spiritu
Intus occultis gubernat procreatrix viribus,
Perque caelum perque terras perque pontum subditum　　　65
Pervium sui tenorem seminali tramite
Imbuit iussitque mundum nosse nascendi vias.

Cras amet qui numquam amavit quique amavit cras amet!

Ipsa Troianos nepotes in Latinos transtulit,
Ipsa Laurentem puellam coniugem nato dedit,　　　　　　70
Moxque Marti de sacello dat pudicam virginem,
Romuleas ipsa fecit cum Sabinis nuptias,
Unde Ramnes et Quirites proque prole posterum
Iulium mater crearet et nepotem Caesarem.

Cras amet qui numquam amavit quique amavit cras amet!　75

Rura fecundat voluptas, rura Venerem sentiunt,

---

59 erit] erat *Scaliger* | quo] quo SV: qui T: quom *Buecheler* || **60** totum] totis STV: totum *Saumaise*: roris *Scaliger* | crearet] creavit S | vernis] vernis STV: vernus *Pithou*: veris *Sanadon* || **61** fluxit] fluctus T | almae] alma et T: almae et V *sed expunxit* et || **62** Unde] ut TV | foetus] flaetus S: fletus T: foetus V aleret] alteret S || **63** venas] vernas T | atque] adque S | mentem] mentem STV: amantum *Schriverius* | permeanti] permeante TV || **64** occultis] ocultis ST | gubernat] gobernat S | procreatrix] procreatis S || **65** Perque] perquem ST | caelum] coelum V | perque¹] perquem S || **66** Pervium] praevium *Baehrens* | tenorem] tenderem S: teporum *Baehrens* || **67** nosse] nosce T || **69** nepotes] nec potes T: penates *Rivinus* | Latinos] latino TV || **70** Ipsa] ipa S || **72** Romuleas] rumuleas T | ipsa] ipsas S: ipsa TV | Sabinis] saumis *vel* sauinis T || **73** Ramnes] Samnes S: rames T: rhamnes V | proque prole] proque prole STV: atque prolem *Shackleton Bailey*: unde prolem *Riese* || **74** Iulium] Romoli ST: Romuli V: Iulium *Davies* | mater] matrem STV: mater *Scaliger*: patrem *Lipsius*: gentem *Riese*: parem *Fort* nepotem] ex nepote *Cameron* || **76** fecundat] facundat T foecundat S ||

*Tomorrow let him love who never has before, and let he who has loved
also love tomorrow!*

Tomorrow is the day on which Aether first took his marriage vows
In order that as a father he might create the whole year from the vernal
    clouds,   60
His fertile rain flowed into the lap of his nurturing wife
From where, mingled with her mighty body, he might rear all his
    offspring.
She, the creatress, with all-pervading spirit and hidden powers
Holds sway within the mind and the veins.
Through the heavens, the earth and seas, all under her control,   65
She infused her penetrating influence by the passage of seed
And she ordered the world to know the ways of birth.

*Tomorrow let him love who never has before, and let he who has loved
also love tomorrow!*

She brought her Trojan descendants into the Latin line,
She gave the girl from Laurentum as a wife to her son,   70
Soon after, she gave the virtuous virgin from the temple to Mars,
She married Romulus' men with the Sabine women,
From which union the mother would create the Ramnes and the
    Quirites
And for the offspring of later generations, Iulius, and his descendant
    Caesar.

*Tomorrow let him love who never has before, and let he who has loved
also love tomorrow!*   75

Delight makes the fields fruitful, the fields feel Venus,

Ipse Amor, puer Dionae, rure natus dicitur.
Hunc ager cum parturiret, ipsa suscepit sinu,
Ipsa florum delicatis educavit osculis.

Cras amet qui numquam amavit quique amavit cras amet!   80

Ecce iam subter genestas explicant tauri latus,
Quisque tutus quo tenetur coniugali foedere;
Subter umbras cum maritis ecce balantum greges
Et canoras non tacere diva iussit alites.
Iam loquaces ore rauco stagna cygni perstrepunt;   85
Adsonat Terei puella subter umbram populi
Ut putes motus amoris ore dici musico
Et neges queri sororem de marito barbaro.
Illa cantat; nos tacemus. Quando ver venit meum?
Quando fiam vel chelidon ut tacere desinam?   90
Perdidi musam tacendo, nec me Phoebus respicit.
Sic Amyclas, cum tacerent, perdidit silentium.

Cras amet qui numquam amavit quique amavit cras amet!

---

77 natus] natu S || **78** parturiret] perturiret TV | sinu] sinum S || **79** delicatis] deligatis
S || **81** subter] super STV: subter *Broukhusius* explicant] explicat STV: explicant
Saumaise | tauri] aonii STV: agni *Lipsius*: apri *Schriverius*: tauri *Scaliger* || **82** tutus] tuus
TV: laetus *Baerhens*: coetus *Lipsius* | tenetur] continetur *Lipsius* | coniugali] cum iugali
T || **83** balantum] valantum T | greges] gregis S: gregum TV: gregis *Lipsius* || **84** canoras]
canores T || **85** stagna] stangna S | cygni] quinni S || **86** Adsonat] adsonate T | Terei]
aerei T | puella] puellae TV subter] supter T | populi] popoli S || **87** putes] putes S *et*
Sannazarius: putas TV | musico] mussico S || **88** Et] Eet T | queri] queris S || **89** Quando]
quan S | ver] vir S | venit] veniet *Jachmann metri causa* || **90** fiam] fiam S: faciam TV: fac
iam *Formicola* | vel] ut STV: uti *Rivinus*: tu *Formicola*: vel *Thomas etiam Bernstein et*
Newton tacere] taceret T || **91** Perdidi ... tacendo] perdidimus an tacendo TV nec] ne
V || **92** Amyclas] amidas T | tacerent] taceret ST | perdidit] perdedit S

Love himself, the son of Dione, is said to have been born in the fields.
When the fields bore him, the goddess took him into her lap,
She raised him on the gentle kisses of flowers.

Tomorrow let him love who never has before, and let he who has loved
*   also love tomorrow!*   80

Look! The bulls are stretching out their flanks under the brooms
Each secure in the conjugal bond by which he is held.
In the shadows, see! the bleating flocks are with their partners,
And the goddess has ordered the birds not to stop their songs.
Now the chattering swans are making the ponds resound with their
    strident voices;   85
Tereus' young wife sings in accompaniment under the shadow of a
    poplar
So that you might think she were singing the emotions of love with her
    tuneful voice
And would deny that she, one of two sisters, was lamenting her cruel
    husband.
She sings, I am silent. When will my spring come?
When will I be like the swallow even, and break my silence?   90
I have lost my muse in staying silent and Phoebus is ignoring me,
Just like silence ruined Amyclae when it stayed silent.

Tomorrow let him love who never has before, and let he who has loved
*   also love tomorrow!*

Commentary

1. *Cras amet qui numquam amavit quique amavit cras amet*

The refrain, repeated eleven times throughout the poem at the beginning of every stanza and at the end of the poem, captures the poem's overall spirit of renewal and regeneration. This is also the theme of stanzas one (lines two to seven) and three (thirteen to twenty-six) in particular. There is no good reason to follow Clementi, Schriverius and Buecheler in moving the refrain from where it stands at the start of the poem: manuscripts S, T, and V all agree on its position. The fact that the refrain begins and closes the poem further enhances its characteristic feeling of renewal and rebirth.

Refrains are employed in various genres throughout classical literature. In Latin poetry it appears in Catullus 61, 62, 64, Vergil, *Eclogues* 8 and Calpurnius Siculus, for example, and in Greek poetry in Theocritus, *Idylls* 1 and 2 alongside the theatrical genres, tragedy and comedy. Notably, in the poetic examples, the refrains are always employed at irregular intervals, as in the *Pervigilium Veneris*.

The refrain immediately introduces the poet's fondness for repetition. Not only is the refrain by its nature repeated, but the words *amo* and *cras* appear twice respectively within the line itself. The next pair of lines will introduce the theme of *ver*, the temporal setting of the poem, using the technique of repetition. Lines such as:

Deque gemmis *deque* flammis *deque* solis purpuris (line twenty-four)

and

Perque caelum *perque* terras *perque* pontum subditum (sixty-five)

also demonstrate the extensive use of repetition elsewhere in the poem. The words *maritus* (in all its forms), *cras,* and *ipsa* are the chief words repeated throughout the poem in addition to *ver.* The words *iubeo* and *amor* – in their nominal, verbal and personified forms – also make a marked appearance, perhaps expectedly, throughout this poem concerning Venus the goddess of love.

The refrain divides the poem into stanzas marking out its progression of thought. This clear development of the ideas in the poem with the refrain, used at once to distinguish the self-contained stanzas and to tie the images in each stanza together, is one of the stronger arguments for accepting the structure of the poem as it stands in the manuscripts (Catlow 1980: 54; Cameron 1984: 212).

2. *Ver novum, ver iam canorum, vere natus orbis est*

This line and the next are indebted to Vergil, *Georgics* 2.323–4:

> Ver adeo frondi nemorum, ver utile silvis,
> Vere tument terrae et genitalia semina poscunt.

The *Pervigilium* expands on the theme of rejuvenation in the plant world and adds a focus on the renewal of amorous feeling in the animal kingdom to Vergil's original image.

vere natus orbis est. For the last part of the line S reads *vere natus iovis est,* while T reads *ver natus orbis est.* Lipsius, who was working with manuscript T alone, conjectured *ver renatus orbis est.* This reading was adopted by Mackail (1912), and more recently by Cameron (1984). Even editors who have not adopted Lipsius's conjecture have recognized its considerable merit, particularly in that it corresponds to the rest of the line by encapsulating an instant response to spring (Catlow 1980: 55). However, the reading that is supported by the other two of the three manuscripts S and V, *vere* *natus*, gives us the pleasing shift from *ver ... ver ... to *vere ... vere ... vere ...* and it also leads the reader into the more general observations about spring which make up the next line.

Editors have drawn a link between *vere natus orbis est* and the doctrines of stoic philosophy (Clementi 1936: 204 and Schilling 1944: 13), but Catlow (1980: 82–3) and more recently Cucchiarelli (2003: 90) convincingly argue that any direct link between this line and stoicism has been overemphasized.

3. *Vere concordant amores, vere nubunt alites*

Vere concordant amores. *Concordare* is rare in the classical era but becomes more frequent in late antiquity after being absorbed into technical legal language (Formicola 1998: 104). At *TLL* 4 87–8; 76.05 *concordo* is recorded under the category *de animantibus*. The *Pervigilium* is cited as an example of this usage. The *amores* here are clearly animate and there is no reason to attempt to translate the words as simply 'love' or 'love-affairs' following Catlow, for example. *Amor* is commonly also used to mean a 'beloved' person (*OLD*), for which compare Vergil, *Eclogues* 10.53–4:

... tenerisque meos incidere amores
arboribus; crescent illae, crescetis, amores

A translation such as 'in spring lovers come together', therefore, not only fits the sense required in the context provided by the parallel phrase *vere nubunt alites* in the second half of the line, but it also makes the best sense of the Latin.

amores ... alites. This line offers the first example of half-rhyme in the poem: *amores ... alites*. There are seven other examples of lines which present this type of internal rhyme at the diaeresis: nine, nineteen, twenty-two, twenty-four, twenty-eight, forty-four and seventy-nine (Currie 1993: 219). To this number should be added the six examples of consecutive rhyme (six and seven, twenty-three and twenty-four, thirty-nine and forty, sixty-nine and seventy, eighty-three and eighty-four, eighty-six and eighty-seven) which also appear in the poem. In early Latin verse and throughout the continued use of the meter, rhyme was a characteristic of the trochaic tetrameter (Sedgwick 1932: 103). Compare, for example Plautus, *Pseudolus* 604–766. Indeed, it has been convincingly argued that rhyme, both internal and consecutive, was used intentionally even in hexameter verse by Vergil and Ovid to underline pauses in sense (Clarke 1972: *passim*). The rhyme that appears in the *Pervigilium* is significant, then, because it places the poem firmly within the tradition of the trochaic tetrameter which stretches as far back as Livius Andronicus and up to Prudentius (Sedgwick 1932: 97–101). To this extent rhyme can certainly be said to be a significant feature of the prosody of the poem. The moderate employment of rhyme in the *Pervigilium* separates the poem somewhat from the style of Mediaeval Latin poetry where use of the technique reached its peak (Norberg 1958: 38).

4. *Et nemus comam resolvit de maritis imbribus*

de maritis imbribus. The use of *de* in the *Pervigilium* is striking and has been noted by nearly all previous editors and commentators. Indeed, Noël-Étienne Sanadon in 1728 attempted to amend away several examples of 'ce malheureux *de* qui a tant défiguré cette pièce', reading on this line for example '*e*' *maritis imbribus*. Catlow (1980: 56) categorizes the thirteen uses of the preposition into groups by their usage: *de loco, de origine, de causa, de relatione*. The poet is most fond of uses of *de origine*, but the most striking is that of *de causa*. All of these usages can be paralleled in the classical authors (see Schilling 1944: xviii) and the use of the preposition cannot therefore be used to date the poem specifically. Indeed, Cameron (1984: 214–15) sees the significance of this word chiefly in its use as a metrical tool. He points out that nearly all the examples begin the second half of a line and that a good deal of the other incidences of the preposition are the product of repetition of the construction.

Even if the poet's partiality for the use of this preposition cannot help us to date the poem or ascribe it concretely to a particular author, it does give the poem an easy and familiar feeling which, when taken with the poet's choice to use the meter of comedy, children's verses and soldiers' songs (Sedgwick 1932: 99), seems significant. This effect is augmented by the use of repetition already identified as a key feature of the poem and the occasional use of prosaic sounding lines: verse eighteen, for example, and thirty-eight. The effect of this familiarizing tendency is to give the poem what has been called 'an air of folk-song' (Catlow 1980: 57) which is set in contrast with the erudite content of the poem and the complex twist at its close. The poet is clearly capable of outstanding literary accomplishment as the substantial bibliography of literary criticism dedicated to the piece attests, along with such achievements of description as line seventeen. The relaxed and popular style of the poem contrasted with the quality of the images and thought in the piece underlines the irony of the poet's view of himself as a poet who has lost the ability to sing (lines eighty-nine to ninety-one), but who has just written one of the most memorable Latin poems of Late Antiquity (for the interpretation of the poem see Introduction).

maritis. The dual sense of the word in this line, at once 'husband' and 'fertile', is part of the richness of its image. The wood unfurls her foliage because of the fertile rains, but at the same time she lets down her hair for her husband, the rains. The poet profits from the same word game at line sixty-one: *in sinum maritus imber fluxit almae coniugis.*

5. *Cras amorum copulatrix inter umbras arborum*

copulatrix. *Copulatrix* does not appear in the classical authors. Even when it is found in the post-classical period it is rare. Interestingly, it is found in Augustine (*On the Trinity* 11.7; 11.9), an author also singled out for his similar use of the preposition *de*, a refrain and a popular style of meter in his *Psalmus contra partem Donati*, a work written to facilitate memorization of the creed by the less educated faithful (Catlow 1980: 57). The psalm's extensive use of *homoioteleuton* – see note on *amores . . . alites* in line three – should also be acknowledged here. While the word *copulatrix* also appears in Ambrosius (*Epistles*, 84), the appearance of this rare word in the *Pervigilium* backed up by the similar stylistic features of Augustine's psalm perhaps points to a northern African provenance and a fourth-century date for the poem. However, the appearance in the poem of the word *procreatrix* (line sixty-four), which also exhibits the agent suffix in *-tor* (*-trix*), means that describing the goddess as *copulatrix* would have required no great feat of creativity from the poet.

6. *Implicat casas virentes de flagello myrteo*

casas virentes. The *casae* are a part of the poet's creation of a ritual atmosphere and setting for the poem. Similar *casae* made of branches appear in Ovid, *Fasti* 3.525–8 in connection with the feast of Anna Perenna, although these huts will conceal a rather different sort of love than those mentioned in the *Pervigilium* (Schilling 1944: xxxviii–ix). Again, Tibullus, 2.1.24 has huts (*turba . . . ex virgis exstruit*), which are part of the festivities at the *Sementivae Feriae*. That the author of the *Pervigilium* intended *casae* (Pithou) not *gazae* (STV) to be woven in the wood is confirmed by line forty-four and the conjecture has therefore been overwhelmingly accepted by later editors.

de flagello myrteo. The myrtle is the sacred plant of Venus, *cf.* Catullus 69.25, Ovid, *Fasti* 4.15 and also Vergil, *Eclogues* 7.62. The myth runs that since the myrtle grows particularly on the shore (*Georgics* 4.124) it sheltered Venus from the prying eyes of the satyrs when she emerged out of the sea (Ovid, *Fasti* 4.139).

7. Cras Dione iura dicit fulta sublimi throno

dicit. *Dicit* is the first example of *praesens pro futuro* in the poem. It is a feature of Late Latin (Rollo 1929: 406–7), which adds to the poem a sense of excitement and expectation for what will take place *cras* 'tomorrow', but also alludes to the fact that spring inevitably comes each year. In this sense the events described in the poem are frequently referred to with a general present since they are customary procedures of the yearly festival that the poem describes. Compare also line fifty-one.

Dione iura dicit. The line establishes Venus in the authoritative role which she assumes throughout the poem. The repetition of the verb *iubeo* on lines twenty-two, twenty-eight, thirty-two (twice), fifty, fifty-six, fifty-seven, sixty-seven and eighty-four – a total of nine times – underlines this function of the goddess which sees her setting down her laws (here and line fifty) and exerting control over the Nymphs, her son Cupid (*Amor*), the whole crowd of festival attendees, and finally the birds in the forest.

Alongside the multiple scenes in which Venus is imagined as a figure of authority, the demonstrative pronoun *ipsa* – used to mark out 'an eminent person' *OLD s.v.* – appears a total of fifteen times in the *Pervigilium* with reference to Venus. It confirms her powerful and revered character throughout the poem. The commanding presence of the goddess lends a sense of order and restraint to the festival which celebrates the act of love (*cf.* note on line six above with regard to the feast of Anna Perenna). This sense of propriety carries through to the descriptions of Venus's role in Rome's history in lines sixty-nine to seventy-four where the rape of the Sabine women and of Rhea Silvia are both described in the context of marriage.

Dione. This is a common epithet of the goddess Venus in Latin poetry (*cf.* Vergil, *Aeneid* 3.19 and Ovid, *Fasti* 2.461 among others). Clementi

(1936: 207–9) gives an extensive account of the mythological roots of this name as a pre-Olympian goddess, a wife of Dodonean Zeus and as the mother of Aphrodite by Zeus. But he also suggests that we can infer something about the character of the goddess in the *Pervigilium* through the use of this name (1936: 72). This conjecture seems unlikely on a number of fronts: in the first place the bacchius *Dĭōnē* suits a trochaic meter much more than the pyrrhic *Vĕnŭs*. Secondly, the use of the Greek synonym for Venus is particularly common in later Latin. It is frequently found, for example, in Tiberianus (1.10) and Sidonius (*Carmina*, 11.173). Finally, the poet himself uses the two names within the poem (*cf.* line thirty-seven: Venus). This ultimately demonstrates the interchangeability of the two names and shows that the author is not using the name of the goddess to refer to a particular mythological tradition.

fulta sublimi throno. *Thronos* is one of a number of graecisms in the *Pervigilium,* including the names of the gods (*Bacchus, Phoebus*), places (*Delos*) and the two common nouns *peplum, chelidon.* The usage of the word *thronos* in Latin is known from Silver Age authors (Pliny, *Historia Naturalis* 35.9, for example). In the modern romance languages, *thronos* would eventually overtake the Latin *solium* (*cf.* French *thrône*, Spanish *trono*, Italian *trono*).

The poetic substitution of *fulta* for *sedens, iacens* or *cubans* has been seen as an example of the use of higher register in the *Pervigilium.* The term appeared *recherché* already in its use at Vergil, *Eclogues* 6.53, where Servius commented that the word seemed antiquated (Smolak 1989: 261 n. 19). It is, however, to be found frequently in Late Antique poetry, especially in Claudian (*cf. De consulatu Stilichonis* 3.199; *Panegyricus dictus Honorio Augusto* 588) (Cucchiarelli 2003: 95).

9. *Tum cruore de superno spumeo pontus globo*

The poet follows Hesiod's account of Venus's birth (*Theogony* 188–97), in which the genitals of Ouranos fall into the sea, having been severed by Kronos. There they are surrounded by foam and it is from this foam that Aphrodite is born. Hesiod differentiates between the ῥαθάμιγγες … αἱματόεσσαι which fall onto the earth (183) and the μήδεα, which fall into the sea (188). Our poet follows what seems to be the Latin tradition in which it is from the blood of the castration that Venus is born (cf. sanguine natam/ Venerem, Tibullus, 1.2 39–40).

Tum. The jump from cras (lines 5, 7 and 8) to tum (here, a time set in mythology) has disturbed many early editors and has been the trigger for many and varied transpositions of verses. Mackail, for example, inserts fifty-nine, Riese inserts thirteen to sixteen, Clementi and Buecheler import fifty-nine to sixty-two (see Clementi pp. 66–8 for a table of all the arrangements of the poem up to his time). Those that do not transpose verses have been inclined to indicate a lacuna – Bergk and Catlow, for example – supposing that the omission occured because the lost line began with another cras, causing the copyist's eye to skip over it (Catlow 1980: 60).

However, in using a temporal marker such as tum the poet has indicated a shift in time back to a fixed mythological past – in illo tempore – which is to be distinguished from the present time and the repeated rituals of spring: 'Insomma, la nascità della dea, nella sua attualità fenomenologica, conserva la sua sacralità nella puntualizzazione temporale, che affonda le radici in un tempo mitico, non calcolabile né ripetibile …' (Formicola 1998: 111). Cazzaniga's elegant emendation tum against the manuscript readings tunc SV and tuno T is adopted here because it removes the deictic suffix (tum)-ce, which is perhaps out of place in referring to a historical myth. Moreover, the word's mutation into tunc/tuno has a simple palaeographical justification since in the uncial and half-uncial letter m the second shoulder and terminal stroke tend to become rounded to the point of resembling an o which would lead either to a rendering as tuno (T) or 'corrected' into tunc (SV).

cruore. Blood is an idea and image integral to the poem. The *cruor*, from which Venus is born, reappears in the rose-virgin stanza on line twenty-three. Here, it is accompanied by a number of further images: *flamma* and *purpor* (twenty-four), *rubor* and *igneus* (twenty-five) which serve to underline the red rose's association with blood. A number of other connections add to the polyvalence of blood's symbolism in the poem: the blood associated with defloration – particularly relevant to the rose-virgin stanza – constitutes a form of sacrifice on the maiden's part. This is, in turn, appropriate to springtime sacrifice mentioned, for example, in Horace's first vernal poem *Carmina*, 1.4.11–12:

> Nunc et in umbrosis Fauno decet immolare lucis
> Seu poscat agna sive malit haedo.

Finally, the red throat of the swallow *hirundo lucida*, a species particularly common in Africa – the likely origin of the *Pervigilium* (see the date and authorship discussion in the Introduction) – connects the theme of red blood to the ambiguity of the final stanza and the poem at large. Blood is, of course, itself an ambiguous image; it is at once a symbol of life and death. The ambiguous symbolism of blood is also to be found at work in the *Pervigilium* when the nymphs seek to keep the wood *incruentum* at line forty (fifty-eight). Here, the blood of unwilling victims from Diana's hunt has a different character from that of the willingly 'sacrificed' victims, or maidens. The prominence of the polysemous blood image in the first half of the poem anticipates the ambiguous image of the swallow, which will dominate the final stanza of the piece. It reveals, already at this early stage in the poem, the double-edged symbolism of spring.

10. *Caerulas inter catervas, inter et bipedes equos*

Caerulas inter catervas. The phrase *caerulas ... catervas* has been identified with the *grex caeruleus Nereidum* of Seneca, *Hippolytus* 335

(Noel 1803) and also the *caerula turba natantum* of Ausonius, *Mosella*, 141 (Schilling 1944: 15).

bipedes equos. This expression can be found at Vergil, *Georgics* 4.388–9. Servius (*ad* 387) helps us to interpret this strange image in his comment on Vergil's line: *equi enim marini prima parte equi sunt, postrema resolvuntur in pisces.*

The dactyl in the sixth foot of this line follows the usual usage of the trochaic tetrameter catalectic (see Introduction, 'Meter'). The poet makes creative use of the meter's flexibilty here to echo the sound of horses' drumming feet. The much expanded use of this technique in *e.g.* Vergil, *Aeneid* 8.596; 8.452 demonstrates the association of the dactyl with the sound of a horse's gait.

11. Fecit undantem Dionem de maritis imbribus

undantem Dionem. The phrase *undantem Dionem* has a triple significance in referring at once to the foaming of the sea where the blood of Ouranos fell; the figure of the goddess rising out of the waves in ` her form as Ἀφροδίτη ἀναδυομένη; and finally the elegant movement of the goddess (*cf.* Apuleius, *Metamorphoses* 2.7).

de maritis imbribus. Suspicion over the MSS reading *de maritis imbribus* is rife. It is possible, of course, that the phrase was copied in error by a scribe who still had the second half of line four in his mind. In this case, as Cucchiarelli notes, a very different original text may have been irrecoverably lost (2003: 99). However, most of the other objections to *maritis*, attested by all manuscripts, stand on unfirm ground: Clementi (1936: 215) complains that '... within the space of fifteen lines the phrase *maritus imber* occurs three times'. It is only in Clementi's own re-arrangement of the verses, however, that this repetition occurs. His second grievance is over the awkwardness of the construction *de cruore fecit Dionem undantem de imbribus*

(I quote here Clementi's paraphrase of the Latin, 1936: 215–16). This awkwardness presumably hinges on the repeated use of the *de* construction which Clementi, in simply adopting Rivinus's conjecture *marinis* for *maritis*, does nothing to obviate.

Catlow (1980: 61) objects in the first place to the adjectival use of *maritus* (see note on line 4). Of course, emending away this usage of *maritus* – which must be taken as an adjective in this line – supports Catlow's argument that the word means only 'husband' in the *Pervigilium* (1980: 11 and 61), so it is easy to see why he is obliged to take Rivinus's *marinis*. In the second place, Catlow argues that *maritis imbribus* is 'no more than an unnecessary, and less precise, reformulation of *cruore de superno spumeo globo*' (61). However, in 1580 Lipsius simply and effectively defended the reading of all three manuscripts and pre-empted the objection that the phrase is an unimaginative repetition: 'maritos imbres *adpellat spumam et cruorem, sane quam eleganter*'. The poet has brought the reproductive elements of the blood and foam together in the word *imbres* and aptly described them as 'fertile', *maritos*.

With suspicion over *maritis* goes the need to emend *imbribus* to *fluctibus* following Sanadon (1728), for example.

13. *Ipsa gemmis purpurantem pingit annum floridis*

Ipsa. The use of the emphatic pronoun throughout the poem to refer to the goddess Venus and thereby signal her power and prominence both in the events of spring and as the primary deity in the piece is another example of the *Pervigilium* poet's repetitive and forceful style.

gemmis purpurantem. The use of the colour of flowers as paint can be found in Lucretius, 5.1395–6. And Apuleius, *Metamorphoses* 10.29,

> Plane tenui specula solabar clades ultimas, quod ver in ipso ortu iam gemmulis floridis cuncta depingeret et iam purpureo nitore prata vestiret

gives us not only a source for the image, but also strong grounds for adopting, as I have done, the conjecture of Rigler, *floridis* for the MSS *floribus*. This reading fits the stylistic mode of the surrounding lines in preserving the suggestive and metaphorical imagery that the poet maintains throughout the stanza. Keeping the MSS *floribus*, after Cazzaniga for example, would require taking the noun in apposition with *gemmis*. This is not only awkward, but it breaks the symbolic imagery of the stanza before it has even begun.

Cucchiarelli keeps the reading of the manuscript tradition *floribus* but, unlike Cazzaniga, defends his choice by the more ingenious reading of the phrases with *gemmis* and *floribus* separately (Cucchiarelli 2003: 101). He takes together *gemmis purpurantem annum*, and then *ipsa pingit floribus* translating as follows: 'Essa l'anno, che si imporpora di gemme, colora di fiori'. This is an attractive reading and it has the virtue of preserving the transmitted text – however untrustworthy the manuscript tradition may be even when it agrees (see *gaz-* STV line six). Moreover, in answer to the oft-quoted passage from Apuleius (*Metamorphoses* 10.29, above), Lucretius 5.1395–6 provides a solid parallel for the phrase *pingere floribus*.

Nevertheless, Cucchiarelli's proposed reading does not overcome the logical and temporal difficulty of having the year turning purple with flower buds (*gemmis purpurantem annum*) at the same time as it is being painted with flowers by Venus (*Ipsa pingit floribus*). If the buds are in the process of emerging, how can Venus be strewing the scene with mature blossoms at the same time? Axt's variation is slightly better, but the causal character he imputes into the phrase is difficult to see in the original Latin as it stands in the MSS.

Rigler's *floridis* is an elegant emendation. It is palaeographically sound, it avoids the awkward apposition of *floribus* and *gemmis*, as well as Axt and Cucchiarelli's division of phrases which, although astute, does not overcome the difficulties of sense in the line.

Purpurare. The verb is only found from the post-classical authors onwards. However, the association of spring with reddening colours is common throughout Classical literature, *cf.* among others Vergil, *Eclogues* 9.40–1: *hic ver purpureum, varios hic flumina circum / fundit humus flores*; alongside *Georgics* 2.319 and Tibullus, 3.5.4.

14. *Ipsa surgentes papillas de Favoni spiritu*

surgentes papillas. The *papillae* form the first image of the metaphor that the poet will construct between the rose and the virgins. The metaphor will be resolved and revealed in line twenty-two where the roses are identified definitely as the naked maids:

> Ipsa iussit mane nudae virgines nubant rosae.

In this line, the *papillae* are the inner, encased blossoms of the roses but also the swelling breasts of a young woman; the *lacrimae* of line seventeen are the drops of dew left by the night air, yet they are also the tears of the virgin who must give herself up to her husband; the *pudor* of line nineteen is at once the head of the folded bud of the rose and the flush of the virgin bride; the loosened *peplus* of line twenty-one is both the robe of the bride-to-be and the calyx of the rose.

The botanical process of the blossoming rose that the *Pervigilium* poet has in mind is explained in Pliny, *Naturalis Historia* 21.14: *Germinat omnis primo inclusa granoso cortice, quo mox intumescente et in virides alabastros fastigato paulatim rubescens dehiscit ac sese pandit in calicem medio sui stantes complexum luteos apices.* The first, closed stage is described here, followed by the swelling of the bud and its eventual reddening before the flower finally opens out into a cup.

The equation of the un-plucked flower and the maiden is also found in Catullus 62, stanza seven where the chorus of maidens explain that as the un-plucked flower gives pleasure to those in a garden, so the maiden is valued by all who surround her, but when the two are 'plucked' they lose their value: *nec pueris iucunda manet, nec cara puellis* (47). This explains the *lacrimae* (seventeen) of the virgins as they prepare for marriage. The image of roses as virgins can be found in the second passage of Apuleius, *Metamorphoses* quoted above (3.29, see note on line thirteen) as well as in other poems included in the *AL* such as 72.8–9.

de Favoni spiritu. The West Wind (*Favonius*, Ζέφυρος) commonly signifies the coming of spring and the blooming of flowers in Classical literature; *cf.* for example, *Homeric Hymn to Apollo* 81–2 and Lucretius 1.11. The particular image in this line may owe something to Catullus 64.282:

Aura parit flores tepidi fecunda Favoni.

15. Urget in nodos patentes; ipsa roris lucidi

nodos. This line, in particular the phrase *nodos patentes,* has received much attention and there exist nearly as many conjectures for the phrase as there are editions of the poem. The manuscripts give us *notos* S; *totos* T V, and *pentes* T; *penates* S V. The reading of S *notos penates* has been preserved by some editors and was most cogently defended by Wernsdorf: '*et* notos penates *interpretor corticem nascentis rosae, quem quasi domicilium suum magis magisque crescendo implet, usque dum pandat se, et in calathum abeat*'. Cazzaniga has provided evidence that *penates* can have the meaning of a dwelling in poetry by reference to *Georgics* 4.153–5 where bees' hives are called *penates* as part of a wider comparison with human society. Certainly it would not be strange for *penates* to be called *notos* in usual circumstances. However, bringing *penates* into the image at this stage mixes the metaphor and makes the line stick out awkwardly in the stanza. Further, virgin roses are being described here which have never blossomed before. A rose bud can only ever blossom once, so describing the next new stage of their blooming process as *notus* 'well-known' or 'familiar' would be odd.

The widely adopted emendation (in Clementi, Schilling and more recently Catlow, Cameron, Formicola and Cucchiarelli) of Schriverius's friend, *nodos*, is accepted here, in the first place because its use with reference to a rose is supported by parallel uses in the Late Antique poetry of the *AL cf.* 72.7, 75.3 and 247.54, for example. There is also evidence of the use of the word with the verbal phrase *urgeo in* at Augustine, *De Ordine* 1.5.14.

> Et roseis crinem nodis subnecte decenter

Codex S (A in Riese's edition) makes the same error, reading *notis* for *nodis*. In this poem, the emendation of S's transmitted reading from *notis* to *nodis* is somewhat surer thanks to the context.

patentes. As for the second word of this corrupted phrase (*pentes* T; *penates* SV), editors have been unsure as to its restoration. The English tradition of scholarship has tended towards *tepentes* (Mackail, Fort, Clementi, Catlow and Cameron), which was first proposed by Lipsius and first taken together with *nodos* by Sanadon. The fullest defence of this reading is offered by Catlow (66). He cites Vergil, *Georgics* 2.330–1: *parturit almus ager Zephyrique tepentibus auris laxant arva sinus*, for the use of *tepens* to describe the West Wind, and Ovid, *Ars Amatoria* 3.185–6 for the adjective applied to spring in general. He suggests that the *nodi* have become *tepentes* by hypallage and sees this as a part of the metaphorical effect in this stanza. The palaeographical support for this reading is explained in full by Clementi (1936: 223), who suggests lipography of the first syllable in T and the addition of a syllable *-a-* in SV.

The reading supported by the Budé editor Schilling is *tumentes*, an emendation suggested by Crusius and most recently printed by Cucchiarelli. Schilling admits that the reading is somewhat weak and offers little in the way of defence. And while Cucchiarelli points to the (not quite) parallel phrasing in *AL* 75: *pyramidas nodo maiore tumentes* (2003: 103), the reading remains palaeographically difficult to justify.

Formicola adopts the reading of Schriverius's friend: *tenaces*. While this adjective makes good sense with *nodus* out of the context of the line – knots tend to be tight and stubborn – it seems a strange notion to introduce to a stanza full of delicate imagery about the unfolding of the roses-*cum*-virgins under a sprinkling of dew in the warm west wind of spring. Formicola's idea of the metaphor being extended to the belt of a virgin's tunic by metonymy of *nodus* is, however, attractive and Vergil, *Aeneid* 1.320 stands in support of the use of the word in this sense. Nonetheless, *tenaces* is difficult to explain from the manuscript testimony. Indeed, Formicola (1998: 118–20) does not attempt such an explanation in his defence of this emendation.

The reading proposed by Wernsdorf in 1782, *patentes*, needs to be revisited. It seems to me to be the most plausible emendation of all those suggested to date. In the first place, *patentes* satisfies the palaeographical requirements just as well as, if not better than, *tepentes* since all MSS attest a word beginning with *p-*. Perhaps a scribe's eye jumped over the *-at-* on account of its similarity to the following *ent-*. Such a jump would be facilitated by the abbreviation of the second syllable to *-ēt-* with the nasal sound indicated by a stroke above the vowel.

Secondly, the phrase *nodos patentes* also makes the best sense at this stage of the stanza. This has been refuted: 'the rose buds should not yet be opening' (Catlow, 1980: 66). However, it is my view that this *is* precisely the moment at which the buds ought to be opening. The poet begins his description of the buds in line thirteen, which extends to half way through this line:

> Ipsa gemmis purpurantem pingit annum floridis
> Ipsa surgentes papillas de Favoni spiritu
> Urget in nodos patentes.

He then switches to a description of the dew in the second half of this line fifteen, focusing on a single drop of dew in minute detail:

> Ipsa roris lucidi,
> Noctis aura quem relinquit, spargit umentes aquas.
> En! Micant lacrimae trementes de caduco pondere:
> Gutta praeceps orbe parvo sustinet casus suos.

Then, all of a sudden, the poet snaps the reader's attention back in line nineteen (*En!*) to the flowers, which have already (perfect tense *prodiderunt*) brought forth their inner bud petals:

> En! pudorem florulentae prodiderunt purpurae.

Were one of the alternative emendations adopted, the crucial moment of the stanza would be missed: the moment when the roses/maidens begin to blossom and surrender their virginity to the Goddess of Love. The poet indicates his intention to underline this critical moment not only with the emphatic *En!* of line nineteen when the flowers have already revealed their *pudores*, but also with the use of enjambement in the current line when the buds are just beginning to open. The technique of enjambement is particularly dynamic here because the reader must carry the subject of the phrase *Ipsa* over the end of the line to its object *nodos patentes* and verb *urget* in the next. The switch to the following image of the dewdrop takes place at the diaeresis, which adds balance and poise to the shift and symmetry of the stanza as a whole.

The poet intended his buds to begin opening here on line fifteen and of the many and various emendations offered by centuries of scholarship no suggestion expresses this more clearly than Wernsdorf's *patentes*, nor with such a plausible palaeographical explanation.

Urget in. Catlow (66) notes that the meaning of *urgeo in*, which has been translated as 'presser de se gonfler' by Schilling for example, and

'to swell into' by Clementi, must mean 'to drive, press into' (*OLD s.v.*).
He is correct. The *papillae* are the hidden inner petals of the rose and
the *nodi* are the encasing buds into which the *papillae* are pressed.
Correctly interpreting the meaning of this line serves to emphasize
the remarkable detail with which the poet is describing the blossoming
of the flower.

roris lucidi. Venus's role as the deity responsible for spreading the
morning dew is elucidated in Pliny, *Naturalis Historia* 2.38: *namque in
alterutro exortu genitali rore conspergens non terrae modo conceptus
inplet, verum animantium quoque omnium stimulat.* In Pliny's account
Venus is conceived in her form as a star, while for the author of the
Pervigilium in this stanza she is imagined sprinkling the moistening
dew as a goddess. Venus is presented in almost all of her guises
throughout the *Pervigilium*; as a cosmic natural force (stanza seven);
as the mother of Rome (stanza eight); as a goddess of flora (stanza
nine); and as a goddess of fauna (stanza ten). The blending of these
conceptions of the goddess, her functions, forms and associated
legends is one of the *Pervigilium*'s great successes and while it is not
necessary to imagine Venus here strictly as the morning star, the
image is by no means out of place.

17. En! Micant lacrimae trementes de caduco pondere

En! Micant. The reading *emicant* for the MSS *et micanat* (S); *et me
canat* (TV) was proposed by Achilles Statius (see Chatelain 1885)
against the alternative emendations, *et micant* (Lispius) and *en micant*
(Schulzius). Statius's emendation has stylistic sensibility on its side.
Lipsius's suggestion *et* seems somewhat superfluous here and the *en*
of Schulzius may detract from the following exclamatory *en* on line
nineteen. In these respects *emicant* would seem to be the best
emendation. However, the philological arguments furnished by
Formicola (1998: 120–1) in support of the simple verb *micant* are

inescapable: The verb *emicare* is not attested with a durative meaning such as is required by the *Pervigilium* here, and the simple form *micare* is often found in the company of adjectives such as *tremulus, tremens,* as in this line of the *Pervigilium.*

The repetition of *en* only two lines later provides no ground on which to dismiss Schulzius's proposal. There is no need to revisit the poet's penchant for this device (for which see the note on line one). Indeed, the double appearance of the exclamation in stanza three lends the passage a pleasing structural framework within which the poet develops his blossoming rose-maiden metaphor.

lacrimae. The connection between *ros* and *lacrima* is common in Latin poetry *cf.* Ovid, *Metamorphoses* 14.708 and Horace, *Ars Poetica* 430 *inter alia.* Indeed, the specific conceit in this line appears also at Ovid, *Metamorphoses* 13.621–2:

> Luctibus est Aurora suis intenta, piasque
> Nunc quoque dat lacrimas et toto rorat in orbe

18. *Gutta praeceps orbe parvo sustinet casus suos*

Catlow (1980: 67) dismisses this line as nothing more than a 'prosaic reformulation of the idea so imaginatively expressed in the previous line'. He notes that *praeceps* here has the meaning 'downward tendency' and that *sustinet* means 'check or restrain'. While Catlow's philological observations are surely correct, his judgement of the role of this line in developing the image of the stanza is less accurate. It is a continuation of the detailed image which follows the bead of dew as it starts to drip from the leaf, maintaining its spherical shape: the dangling dew-bead just checks its fall.

This interpretation of the line is supported by Pliny's description of liquid's tendency to form into circular droplets. This reference has not been noted by previous scholarship. The lines in Pliny read:

namque et dependentes ubique guttae parvis globantur orbibus et pulveri inlatae frondiumque lanugini inpositae absoluta rotunditate cernuntur (*Naturalis Historia* 2.65.163). The passage not only provides a parallel for the vocabulary used in the *Pervigilium*, it also supports the idea behind the image that the *Pervigilium* poet has in mind: the dew drops form and maintain spherical droplets as they hang and fall from the leaves and petals of the roses.

19. En! Pudorem florulentae prodiderunt purpurae

En! The manuscripts read *in* at the start of this line. Bouhier first saw that this concealed *en!* emphatically calls the reader's attention to the fact that the roses have brought out their inner petals and the maidens have blushed at the thought of the festival bringing them into womanhood. See note on line fifteen for the role of this exclamation in the poet's description of the process of the opening of the rose.

florulentae. The word is a neologism and synonym of the classical *florens,* or *floridus.* The creation of adjectives in *-ulentae-* is found often in Plautus and, after a fall in usage amongst the classical authors, it occurs frequently again in Apuleius and later (Formicola 1998: 122). The form *florulentus* is not attested before the fourth century (see *TLL* 6.1.926–7 *s.v.*), a fact that weighs in favour of a later dating for the poem.

Lines nineteen and twenty have been frequently identified with Fulgentius, *Mitologicae* 1.11–12. The resonance is striking:

> Ubi guttas florulentae mane rorat purpurae,
> Umor algens quem serenis astra sudant noctibus.

20. Umor ille, quem serenis astra rorant noctibus

The association between dew and the flowering of the rose had been a theme in Classical literature since at least Sappho (Voigt 96 / Diehl 98, 12–13):

ἀ δ᾽ ἐέρσα κάλα κέχυται, τεθά-
λαισι δὲ βρόδα κἄπαλ᾽ ἄν-
θρυσκα καὶ μελίλωτος ἀνθεμώδης.

This connection is also noted by Cucchiarelli (2003: 105).

21. Mane virgineas papillas solvit umenti peplo

virgineas. Lipsius emended *virgineas* ST to *virgines* V (without knowledge of V) presumably to avoid a dactyl in the second foot, but a dactyl has already occurred in line 17 *lacrimae*. See the discussion of meter in the Introduction.

solvit. The tense of *solvit* is ambiguous. It should be read as a present tense in an idomatic instance of the *praesens pro futuro* since the adverb *mane* 'in the morning' at the beginning of the line requires this sense.

umenti. S reads *tumenti* which is an error through dittography, T does the opposite and transfers the final *-t* of *solvit* onto *umenti*. Manuscript V preserves the correct reading (*h*)*umenti*.

peplo. is another of the poem's hellenisms (see also *thronos* line seven and *chelidon* line ninety, for example). It stands at once for the robe of the virgin and the calyx of the rose. The word was used especially for a robe dedicated to Minerva and was later applied more broadly to any fine clothing (see *OLD s.v.*). The image of the loosened robe in this line can also be found in *AL* 72.8:

Necdum virgineus pudor exsinuatur amictu

22. Ipsa iussit mane totae virgines nubant rosae

mane totae. Discussion has centred on the word *totae* in this line. The manuscripts read respectively: *manet tute* S; *mane tuae* T; *mane tute* V. Emendations have been many and varied. The most frequently adopted have been Achilles Statius's *mane ut udae*; Mackail's *mane nudae*; Scaliger's *mane tutae* and Orelli's *mane totae*.

The construction *iubeo ut* ... was put under suspicion by Mackail, who considered the construction ungrammatical. Owen (1893) showed that the construction, although rare, exists in Latin, citing Livy 28.36 among other examples in support. In the *Pervigilium*, however, *iubere* is followed by an infinitive – the more common construction – every other time it occurs (lines twenty-eight, thirty-two, forty-nine, fifty-five, fifty-six, sixty-seven, eighty-four). Moreover, Catlow's argument that the phrase *udae virgines* 'conveys a notion of concupiscence which is foreign to the emotional context of the stanza' is very convincing, especially when taken with the *Pervigilium*'s mollification of the mythological rape of Rhea Silvia by Mars and of the Sabine women by the Romans in the antepenultimate stanza of the poem (see note on line seven).

The sense of Scaliger's *tutae* 'safe', 'protected', is incongruous at this stage in the poem, particularly when we have the image of maidens' tears contained in the metaphor running throughout the stanza.

The proposal *nudae* has been accepted by Clementi and Catlow. It is tempting to hold up the mirror to Catlow's own dismissal of Orelli's conjecture (*totae*) and reflect the sentiments of Formicola, who considers *nudae* 'in verità piuttosto banale e flaccido nel contesto'. But the palaeographical evidence provides a more solid case for discarding the emendation. Catlow presents the case of *nodos* in line fifteen as justification for adopting *nudae* here, 'By a similar process of confusion *nudae* has resulted in *tute*' and although it is easy to see how the medial dental sounds became confused as well as the diphthong at the end of the word, it is somewhat more of a stretch to see from where the initial *n* comes in this line. In the example from line fifteen the dental sound could have ended up in the initial position in MSS T and V by anticipation of writing it at the start of the second syllable. If nothing else, the letter *n* appears at the start of the word in MS S. In the present line, however, there is no hint of a nasal sound in the word in any of the manuscripts, and in the hands of T and V there is a clear gap between *mane* and *totae*, as well as in S which for the most part does not separate words. This suggests that the scribes recognized the words as separate, thereby protecting *totae* from contamination with the nasals in *mane*.

Orelli's reading *totae* (1831) balances the surviving manuscript evidence with a satisfying meaning in the line. On the first count, the confusion of the back vowels -*u*- and -*o*- takes place elsewhere in the *Pervigilium* codd. *e.g.* at line fifty-four *locus* S and *locos* T for *lucos* (supported by V). This would explain *tu*- for -*to*-. As for the meaning, *totus* for 'all' arises as a feature of post-Classical Latin. Compare, for example, Apuleius, *Metamorphoses* 3.24; 3.28 and 4.14. Moreover, the word appears a further two times in the *Pervigilium* (lines fifty-one and sixty) with this meaning.

23. *Facta Cypridis de cruore deque Amoris osculis*

Cypridis. The manuscripts' iamb *prius* does not fit the meter in this line. I follow Buecheler (1859), Mackail (1912) Rand (1934) and more recently Shackleton Bailey (1982), Cameron (1984) and Cucchiarelli (2003) in reading *Cypridis* in its place. The reading is supported by the evidence of *AL* 73.2–3:

> ...aut sentibus haesit
> Cypris et hic spinis insedit <s>anguis acutis

Venus was often referred to by the name of the island that claimed her birth. Compare, for example, Tibullus, 3.3.34, where she is called *Cypria*.

It is interesting to note that in line seventy-nine of the poem *Amor* is said to have been brought up on roses' kisses. In the poet's mind the relationship seems to have been mutually beneficial.

25. Cras ruborem, qui latebat veste tectus ignea

ruborem. *Rubor* here is synonymous with *pudor* (line nineteen). This parallelism has been taken so literally that Baehrens changed the reading to *pudorem* and then read *rudebit* for *pudebit* in the next line. The word refers to both the blushing virginity of the maiden and the opening inner petals of the rose. Cicero, *Tusculanae Disputationes* 4.19 demonstrates the relationship of *rubor* and *pudor* in a Stoic setting: *ex quo fit ut pudorem rubor . . . consequatur.*

veste . . . ignea. The *veste ignea* suggests the *flammeum* – the Roman wedding veil: *cf.* Martial, 11.78.3 *flammea texuntur sponsae.* Within the rose-maiden metaphor the *veste ignea* also represents the deep red outer petals of the rose head.

26. Unico marita nodo non pudebit solvere

Unico. Pithou emended the MSS *unica* ST; *unica(at)* V to *unico* in the *editio princeps* of 1578. It has been very widely accepted. A rival reading was proposed by Wernsdorf (1785) who suggested *uvido*, but the metaphor which started the stanza weighted towards images of the flower has itself 'blossomed' so to speak and now refers more directly to the maidens. Furthermore, it is more plausible to imagine that an error of *homoioteleuton* with the next word *marita* (SV) has occurred here rather than the substitution of a word with an entirely different sense.

nodo. Two strong alternatives have been proposed for the MSS readings *nodo* (TV), *noto* (S). Bergk offered *voto* in 1859, recently accepted by Cucchiarelli. Buecheler, also 1859, proposed *Noto* (the South Wind). Bergk's suggestion offers a very clear sense and the palaeographical mechanics of the error are easy to see. However, the reading of TV is more plausible for three reasons: firstly MS S has confused the dental sound in this word before in line fifteen as well as in other poems throughout the *AL* (see note to line fifteen). After adjusting for this simple error, the MSS are unanimous on the reading *nodo*. Secondly, if *voto* is accepted all the metaphorical imagery of the stanza disappears in the final line. The passage is more satisfying if the figurative language is sustained until the end – especially if the reading in line fifteen is correct – since it is clear that our poet would not be averse to repeating the word. Finally, and unrecognized until this edition of the *Pervigilium*, the line describes the ritual untying of the *nodus Herculaneus*, the knot tied around the waist of the bride at a Roman wedding:

> Cingillo nova nupta praecingebatur, quod vir in lecto solvebat, factum
> ex lana ovis, ut, sicut illa in glomos sublata coniuncta inter se sit, sic vir
> suus secum cinctus vintusque esset.
>
> Festus, 55L, s.v.

The knot was tied with the ends of a woolen *cingulum* or belt and represented the bride's chastity. Before the knot was tied, the wool was twined into a cord to represent the strong bond of the bride and groom. It was to be undone (*solvere*) only by the husband in the marriage bed (Bonfante 1994: 48). Knots of a similar nature are also found in the Augustan poets although they are not connected with marriage and rather with love-spells or dedications. Compare for example, Vergil, *Eclogues* 8.76–8:

> Ducite ab urbe domum, mea carmina, ducite Daphnin.
> Necte tribus nodis ternos, Amarylli, colores,
> necte, Amarylli, modo, et 'Veneris' dic 'vincula necto.'

The proposal of Buecheler is attractive, 'the maiden-rose will not be ashamed to reveal her blush to (at the touch of) the South Wind alone'. However, the reading requires changing the word order to *unico Noto marita* for the sake of the meter and such a change is unwarranted.

pudebit. The evidence for *pudeo* as a personal verb is rare but attested; it appears at Plautus, *Casina* 877 and Lucan, 8.495, see *TLL s.v.*

non pudebit solvere. In other poems that compare the surrender of virginity to the plucking of a flower, the scene frequently ends with assertions of violation, sexual pleasure or the brevity of youth *cf.*:

> Sic virgo, dum intacta manet dum cara suis est,
> Cum castum amisit polluto corpore florem,
> Nec pueris iucunda manet nec cara puellis
>
> Catullus, 62.45–7

> Necdum virgineus pudor exsinuatur amictu,
> Ne pereant, lege mane rosas: <cito> virgo senescit.
>
> *AL*, 72.8–9

These passages are cited by Catlow in his good discussion of the Rose Stanza (1980: 62–4). He concludes by observing that in the *Pervigilium* the blossoming of the rose and the surrender of virginity do not represent a loss but a dedication to Venus, which is a part of womanhood. This theme can be taken further by connecting the delicate treatment of the rose's maturation and the positive assertion of the submission of virginity to the image of Venus presented throughout the poem. The Venus of the *Pervigilium* presides over the 'marriage' of Rhea Silvia to Mars and of Romulus's men to the Sabine women (stanza eight); she warns the nymphs to be wary of *Amor* (Cupid) and his tricks (stanza four) and she is given a strong and powerful image throughout the poem which is emphasized by the repeated use of the verb *iubeo* and the pronoun *ipsa cf.* note on line seven. This is quite the opposite of the standard image of Venus in lyric poetry. Compare:

> Audendum est: fortes adiuvat ipsa Venus.
> Illa favet seu quis iuvenis nova limina temptat
> Seu reserat fixo dente puella fores;
> Illa docet molli furtim derepere lecto,
> Illa pedem nullo ponere posse sono

Illa viro coram nutus conferre loquaces
Blandaque compositis abhere verba notis.

Tibullus, 1.2.16–22

Here Venus, although still a figure of authority (note the repeated *illa* and her role as *doctor* in lines nineteen to twenty-two), is using her power for very different purposes. She teaches lovers how to manage secret trysts and to communicate under the nose of the paramour's husband. This is quite opposed to the Venus of the *Pervigilium* who commands the maidens to *nubere* (wed), maidens who are not ashamed to reveal their *rubor* as wives. The character of the love goddess and the relationships described in the *Pervigilium* are of an honest and even moral type. This gentle description of the rose blossoming combined with the face of Venus that is presented throughout the poem translates this to the reader.

solvere. For this usage of *solvere* see Catullus, 61.51. But note, with reference to the point made above, that in Catullus the bride is warned:

Nupta, tu quoque, quae tuus
Vir petet, cave ne neges,
Ni petitum aliunde eat.

Catullus, 61.147–9

This example demonstrates the key difference between the *solutio* in the *Pervigilium* and that required in Catullus 61.

28. *Ipsa nymphas diva luco iussit ire myrteo*

luco iussit ire. The dative of motion towards used with *ire* is a feature of Augustan poetry. Compare, for example, Vergil, *Aeneid* 5.451: *it clamor caelo*.

myrteo. For the association between Venus and the myrtle see the note on line six.

29. *It puer comes puellis, nec tamen credi potest*

It. Nearly four-hundred and fifty years ago Lipsius read *it* for the MSS *et*. In support of this reading compare the frequency of the phrase *comes ire* in the classical poets (see Formicola: 133 for no fewer than nine examples, among which are Vergil, *Aeneid* 6.448; Tibullus, 1.4.41). Lipsius's reading has been unanimously adopted by modern editors.

puer. The role of the *puer* (*Amor*) in the *Pervigilium* is set in contrast to that of Venus. Cupid plays his role as the cheeky and dangerous youth, while Venus cautions: *nymphae cavete quod Cupido pulcher est* (34). This gives a new dynamic to the relationship of mother and son who usually operate in tandem. This contrast serves to underline the respectable image of Venus throughout the *Pervigilium*, for which see the note on line twenty-six.

The image of Cupid with his bow, torch, quiver and love arrows is Alexandrian in origin (Schilling 1944: liii). But in stanza nine, which links Venus to the earth's fruitfulness, the poet tells us the story of *Amor*'s birth from the fields. This story only exists in the Latin tradition and can be found at Tibullus, 2.1.67–8 *inter alia*:

> Ipse quoque inter agros interque armenta Cupido
> Natus et indomitas dicitur inter equas.

The second half of this line, '*nec tamen credi potest . . .*', alongside lines thirty-four and fifty-seven maintain the ambiguous or mistrustful image of the god *Amor*. While the image of Cupid throughout the stanza is kept light and playful – he is *feriatus* and *nudus* – the poet maintains the idea of the threat he offers to the security of the festival and the maidens: *totus est armatus idem quando nudus est Amor* (line thirty-five).

30. *Esse Amorem feriatum, si sagittas vexerit*

sagittas vexerit. In 1637 Saumaise objected to the use of *veho* in the sense of carrying weapons calling it an '*idiotismus illius aevi quo vixit auctor* Pervigilii'. However, the usage of the word as a synonym of *fero*, *porto* or *gesto* is known from Augustan poetry: compare Horace, *Sermones* 1.1.48, where *veho* is used for carrying bread on the shoulder.

31. *Ite nymphae, posuit arma, feriatus est Amor*

posuit arma. The first foot of the second metron is resolved into a tribrach. For *Arma ponere* and its implications for the image of Cupid presented in this stanza see note on line twenty-nine. *Amor* was also asked to surrender his weapons at Tibullus, 2.1.81–2:

> Sancte, veni dapibus festis, sed pone sagittas,
> Et procul ardentes hinc, precor, abde faces.

32. *Iussus est inermis ire, nudus ire iussus est*

inermis ire, nudus ire. The two halves of the line (*inermis ire, nudus ire*) are balanced in a chiastic pattern with their governing verbs, which lends a clear sense of balance to the line. A similar technique was employed at lines thirty and thirty-one where the phrases *esse Amorem feriatum* and *feriatus est Amor* are placed at the start and end of the lines respectively.

nudus. The association between 'naked' *nudus* and 'unarmed' *inermis* is a common *jeu de mots* which is also found in lines thirty-five and fifty-seven. To compare here is Ovid, *Ars Amatoria* 1.2.38.

33. *Neu quid arcu, neu sagitta, neu quid igne laederet*

Neu . . . neu . . . neu. The poet has a fondness for verbal repetition, for which see note to line one. The *deque . . . deque . . . deque* of line twenty-four and *perque . . . perque . . . perque* of line sixty-five are other examples of the same tricolon repetition. The piling up of the negative conjunctions here serves to echo the ambiguous reputation of young Cupid throughout mythology (Formicola 1998: 135). It also highlights the threat that his presence could potentially pose to the festival if his mother did not have him under control; see *puer* in line twenty-nine.

35. *Totus est armatus idem quando nudus est Amor*

armatus. In the place of *armatus* the manuscripts read *inermis* (STV). *Inermis* gives the opposite sense to that which is required in this stanza. The most obvious emendation from *inermis* is *in armis*, which Pithou provided in the *editio princeps* of the poem in 1578. Unfortunately *in armis* does not scan since it introduces a spondee into the third foot. Several solutions have been concocted to circumvent this problem: in 1637 and 1638 respectively, Saumaise and Schriverius suggested that the word order be changed to *est in armis totus idem* . . . and in 1644 Rivinus proposed *totus haud inermis*. Some scholars have even found ways to retain the reading of the codd.: Mackail, followed similarly by Fort, translated the line as 'Love naked is complete, Love unarmed is the same'; Ussani and more recently Formicola make the line into a question: 'Is love completely harmless even when naked?'

None of these solutions is without troubling flaws: the rearrangement of Saumaise and Schriverius requires us to make the assumption that 'lightning has struck twice in the same place' (Courtney 2005: 401); that *in armis* was mistaken for *inermis* and then that *totus* was omitted and replaced in the wrong position. It is hardly a desirable situation when one is obliged to emend an emendation. Rivinus's suggestion stands on no palaeographical basis: *haud* for *est* is a difficult change to justify. Mackail has to force the Latin into a very awkward mould to achieve his meaning, even if one could accept his rendering of the line 'on prêterait une tautologie au poète' (Schilling 1944: 19). Inserting a question at this point does not fit with the very affirmative character of the stanza (note the imperative at lines thirty-one and thirty-four as well as the double use of *iubeo* in line thirty-two); any ambiguity could have been dealt with by the poet in reading something like *estne* (Clementi 1936: 232) which, indeed, would scan.

In light of these considerations, the conjecture offered by Courtney (2005), *armatus*, is the most convincing. This reading has, in the first place, the benefit of providing the required meaning for the line. *Armatus* also fits the metrical requirements. Moreover, Courtney provides a solid paleographical explanation for his proposal: a scribe, coming to the word *est*, flicked his eyes up to the similarly positioned *est* on line thirty-two (two syllables into the line and following the ending *-us*); he then proceeded to copy out the following word (*inermis*) before returning to this line (thirty-five), an error *d'un saut du même au même* (Havet 1911: 130). This is one of the more common copying errors and one which allows the critic to leave behind the concern for finding a word similar in appearance to that found in the manuscripts. Elegant in its relative simplicity and suitability for the line, the emendation also has some aesthetic qualities that Courtney does not admit. The balance of *est armatus* with *nudus est* is reminiscent of the similar chiastic technique noted on line thirty-two and between lines thirty and thirty-one (see note on line thirty-two). The poise of *Totus* at the start of the verse and *Amor* at the end helps to round off the line and indeed the stanza.

37. ʿConpari Venus pudore mittit ad te virgines

Conpari. The speech of the virgins begins with this line. Reading the line in this way, as the beginning of the virgin's appeal to Diana, removes the need to indicate a lacuna after the refrain following Riese. By opening with the word *conpari* the virgins instantly communicate to Diana that they are approaching her as equals in respect of their virginity. Later, the poet will set Diana and the virgins in immediate contrast because the virgins, although *conpari pudore* as they make their request to the hunting goddess, will not be so after the festival.

38. *Una res est quam rogamus: cede virgo Delia*

Delia. The epithet *Delia* for *Diana* is well attested in Classical Latin poetry (*cf. inter alia* Horace, *Carmina* 4.6.33 and Vergil, *Eclogues* 7.29). The epithet comes from her birthplace, Delos, although another tradition (see *Homeric Hymn to Apollo*, 16) has her born in Ortygia. The contrast between Diana the virgin goddess and Venus the goddess of love and sex is already present in the *Homeric Hymn to Aphrodite* (16–17):

οὐδέ ποτ᾽ Ἀρτέμιδα χρυσηλάκατον, κελαδεινὴν
δάμναται ἐν φιλότητι φιλομμειδὴς Ἀφροδίτη.

Here, as in the *Pervigilium*, Diana (Artemis) cannot be swayed from her chastity.

Una res est quam . . . The language of this phrase is prosaic and reminiscent of spoken language (Formicola 1998: 139). This serves as another indicator to the reader that the poem is entering direct speech after the refrain.

39. *Ut nemus sit incruentem de ferinis stragibus*

de. Note the idiomatic use of the preposition *de* in this line, see note on line four.

40. *Et rigentibus virentes ducat umbras floribus* (58)

The transposition of line fifty-eight to the position of line forty (in the text offered here) was first proposed by the anonymous Leipzig editor of 1872 and has been widely accepted. The line makes no sense in its position in all three manuscripts at line fifty-eight. Further to this, I follow Cameron and Catlow in rejecting Scaliger's *recentibus* for the MSS *rigentibus*. Maintaining the transmitted reading supports the case for moving the line to this position, since when Diana leaves the woods the *flores* will remain *rigentes*, 'upright' or 'untrampled', by the hunt. Transposition of this verse to line forty also explains the *et* which begins the line as well as the subjunctive of *ducat* which follows *Ut nemus* ... in the previous verse. Editors who have moved the verse to other positions (Riese moved it to follow line fifty-two, and Martin (1935) moved all of fifty-eight to sixty-two to follow line seven for example) have had to emend the line to make it fit the syntactical context. Riese changed *et* to *ut* and Martin had to change *ducat* to the indicative *ducit*. Other editors avoid the problem altogether by indicating a lacuna (Trotski, Schilling, and Cazzaniga). Indeed, Schilling's only objection (22) to the transposition of the line to this position rests on the adoption of Scaliger's emendation, without which the verse fits the context very well indeed.

Another proposed transposition which carries the same benefit as the transposition adopted in my text, that of not having to emend the line after moving it, is Formicola's suggestion (146–7) to place the line between verses forty-eight and forty-nine. He argues that the subjunctive mood of *ducat* follows the subjunctive of *regnet* in line forty-eight and he retains the MSS reading *rigentibus*. The real strength of this proposed move is the palaeographical defence which argues that an error of *homoioteleuton* with line fifty caused the line to be omitted and then re-inserted in the wrong position. However, the same defence has been offered for the transposition to line forty by Cameron (1984: 225), with *un saut du même au même* suspected between the endings of *strag-ibus* and *flor-ibus*. Cameron's argument has the additional benefit of not having to deal with the awkward appearance of the refrain in the middle of the suspected *homoioteleuton* as must Formicola. This puts the two suggestions on a level playing field since Formicola's proposed *saut* has the advantage of being between two examples of the same word rather than just between the same endings. The sense supplied by the transposition adopted here seems to me stronger than that offered by Formicola since line forty-eight:

> Regnet in silvis Dione, tu recede Delia!

offers an emphatic and satisfying way to finish the appeal to Diana to quit the woods. If line fifty-eight is appended onto the end of this stanza this effect disappears and the stanza finishes with the much less decisive call for the flowers to be left upright.

41. *Ipsa vellet te rogare si pudicam flecteret*

Manuscript T omits this line probably on account of *homoioarchon* with line thirty-four. The remaining two manuscripts which have transmitted the line read *erogare* which would make very little sense here. Saumaise corrected this to *te rogare*. The error clearly came about due to haplography of the final *-t* in *vellet*.

42. *Ipsa vellet ut venires si deceret virginem*

vellet. The change in construction from *volo* with the infinitive to *volo* with *ut* gives a liveliness to the lines. It is also a logical progression because the two lines share the same subject.

43. *Iam tribus choros videres feriatis noctibus*

feriatis. ST and V all read *feriatis*. Pithou proposed *feriatos* presumably to avoid having the participle agree with the impersonal *noctibus*. Schriverius suggests *feriantis* for the same reason. Neither of these emendations is necessary or desirable since the use of *feriatus* is well known with impersonal nouns *cf.* Pliny, *Epistolae* 3.14.6, among others: *dies feriatus*.

44. *Congreges inter catervas ire per saltus tuos*

Congreges. A rare post-classical word, although it is found in Apuleius (Catlow 1980: 78).

45. Floreas inter coronas, myrteas inter casas

myrteas inter casas. Callimachus's *Hymn to Artemis* provides an explanation of Diana's dislike for the myrtle plant. The poem tells the story of one of the goddess's nymphs, Britomaris, who was fleeing from the lusty pursuit of Minos when the myrtle hindered her escape:

μύρτοιο δὲ χεῖρες ἄθικτοι:
δὴ τότε γὰρ πέπλοισιν ἐνέσχετο μύρσινος ὄζος
τῆς κούρης, ὅτ᾽ ἔφευγεν: ὅθεν μέγα χώσατο μύρτωι.

(201–4)

46. Nec Ceres, nec Bacchus absunt nec poetarum deus

Ceres … Bacchus … poetarum deus. The presence of these three gods (Ceres, Bacchus and Apollo) at the festival has been used to support an African origin for the poem. Schilling (1944: 20) cites Vergil, *Aeneid* 4.58 where Dido makes a sacrifice to the same three gods. However, Ceres and Bacchus are called to the festival in Tibullus, 2.1.3–4:

> Bacche, veni dulcisque tuis e cornibus uva
> Pendeat, et spicis tempora cinge, Ceres.

Indeed, the relationship between Venus (the god at the centre of the *Pervigilium*), Bacchus and Ceres is proverbial, as has been most recently noted by Cucchiarelli (2003: 116):

> sine Cerere et Libero friget Venus.

The proverb is quoted by Terence, *Eunuchus* 4.5.6 and repeated by Cicero, *De Natura Deorum* 2.23.60. The poet of the *Pervigilium* himself explains Apollo's (*poetarum deus*) appearance in the next line. This is the first hint in the poem of the poetical concerns of the author which will be brought to the fore in the final stanza of the poem. The litotes used to introduce the three gods in the *Pervigilium* serves to underline the importance of their presence at the festival. It should also be remarked that the emphasis is on the attendance of Apollo both by virtue of his position at the end of the line and the periphrastic manner in which he is named. Indeed, this periphrasis itself serves to highlight the quality of the god in which the poet is most interested and which will be the core of his appeal at the end of the poem.

47. *Detinenda tota nox est, pervigilanda canticis*

Detinenda. Debate centres on the words *detinenda* and *pervigilanda* in this line. In the case of the first word, the manuscripts have transmitted *detinente* S and *detinent et* TV. The simple emendation from Heinsius, *detinenda*, gives good sense, has a plausible palaeographical explanation and provides a pleasant balance of gerundives in the line. For the sense of *detineo* in this line, Clementi (1936: 238) provides a good example from Ovid, *Metamorphoses* 1.682–3:

Euntem multa loquendo detinuit sermone diem

which demonstrates the usage of the word with *dies*. A parallel usage with *nox* cannot be too much of a stretch. The substitution of dentals in the manuscripts is frequent (see note on line fifteen for example) and similar vowel sounds are frequently confused as well *cf. vellit* for *vellet* (lines forty-one to forty-two) in S and *loco* for *luco* (line twenty-eight) in TV. This would explain how *detinenda* became *detinente* in S, and dittography of the following initial consonant would explain the appearance of *-t* in TV. With these arguments it is hard to find the 'difficoltà per motivi paleographici' that Formicola has seen (1998: 144) or how the emendation is 'superfluo e fuori luogo' (*ibid.*).

As is the case with any difficult *locus* in the *Pervigilium* alternative conjectures abound: Schenkl and Baerhens read *detinenter*, which, while keeping close to the transmitted text of the MSS, has scant evidence as an adverb in Latin. Catlow (1980: 78) shuns Cazzaniga's *continenter*, adopted notably by Shackleton Bailey, as 'ridiculous'. This is harsh criticism because the sense would be quite appropriate to the line if the palaeographical justification were not so difficult. The same goes for Formicola's offering: *quod decenter* which he defends by proposing that the majuscule *quod* was abbreviated to *Q* which was then confused with the following *D* and omitted through haplography. Even if this convoluted process might have taken place, it would still leave us with some gap between *decenter* and *detinente*. The *te sinente* of Prasch, Sanadon and Bouhier has been rejected for exactly the opposite reason: the palaeography is easier, but the sense is awkward. It is hard to explain why the nymphs, who are about to order Dione to leave (*cede!*) in the next line, would be asking her to permit the presence of these gods here. Another popular emendation adopted by Saumaise, Wernsdorf and Mackail is *de tenente*. This phrase could be supported by analogy with the similar idiom 'd'un tenant' in French, but there are no Latin parallels.

pervigilanda. The word comes down through the manuscripts as *perviclanda* S: *pervigila* T: *pervigil a* V. The uncontracted form of the word conforms to standard metrical practice as Catlow (1980: 79) has noted.

48. *Regnet in silvis Dione, tu recede Delia*

The line exemplifies the fondness for parallelism which the author of the *Pervigilium* demonstrates throughout the poem. This feature of the style and structure of the piece has been studied at some length (Currie 1993: 215–20) and is an indicator of the poem's proximity to popular Latin style in some of its features including the choice of meter, vocabulary and occasional use of prosaic phrasing. Currie identifies three types of parallelism: synonomous, antithetical and synthetic. The *Pervigilium* demonstrates examples of all of these varieties of parallelism, *cf.* line thirty-two for the synonomous kind, the refrain and the current line for examples of the antithetical parellelism along with line forty-seven for synthetic, for example.

50. *Iussit Hyblaeis tribunal stare diva floribus*

Hyblaeis. Clementi (1936: 239–41) presents the argument for associating the Hybla of the *Pervigilium* with the town of Hybla Gereatis on the southern slopes of Aetna, now the modern day Sicilian town of Paternò. However sensible Clementi's identification of the town may be, the mention of Hybla in the *Pervigilium* serves more to set the poem in the proverbially fecund landscape of Latin literature than in any precise geographical location. The sweetness of this literary setting is attested *inter alia* at Vergil, *Eclogues* 1.54; 7.37; Martial, 2.46.1–2; 11.42.3 through to Claudian, *De raptu Proserpinae* 2.79–80 and even in the *Carmina Burana*, 119.13. In the *Pervigilium* Hybla is literally surrounded by flowers: in the current line *Hyblaeis … floribus*; in line fifty-two *Hybla totos funde flores* and fifty-three *Hybla florum sume vestem*.

tribunal. The word here refers back to the *sublimi throno* of line seven. Technically the *tribunal* is used for the raised platform of judges, but here Venus will be presiding over love matches. Formicola (1998: 151) remarks on the humour in this image; the poet has his tongue in his cheek in the use of this word and it gives an air of levity and gaiety to the lines.

51. *Praeses ipsa iura dicit, adsederunt Gratiae*

Praeses. The MSS read *praesens* which would introduce a spondee into the first foot. Scaliger corrected the word to *praeses* which not only solves the metrical issue but fits the sense of the line since Venus is the person presiding over the *tribunal* and also the guardian of the festival and the lovers.

adsederunt. Many editors have attempted to emend away what they saw as a metrical error introducing a spondee into the fifth foot. However, see the metrical discussion and the examples in the note on line forty-seven for the fallacy of this assertion. The juxtaposition of the present *dicit* and the perfect *adsederunt* has also provided grounds to emend the line, and the conjecture of Dousa Filius: *dicet* ... *adsidebunt* has been widely accepted (see the editions of Shackleton Bailey and Schilling, for example). However, the sense of expectancy and excitement gained in the line by retaining the manuscript reading *adsederunt* – the Graces have already sat down – along with the similar effect achieved by the use of the *praesens pro futuro* in *dicit* (already noted as a feature of the poem in line seven) are strong arguments for keeping the reading of the MSS (Cucchiarelli 2003: 119).

Gratiae. The Graces and nymphs are associated with Venus in one of Horace's spring poems, *Carmina*, 1.4.5–7, and commonly appear in her retinue elsewhere *cf.* Homer, *Odyssey* 18.193–4 and the *Homeric Hymn to Apollo*, 194–6.

iura dicit. The image of a legal setting is continued in this line from *tribunal* in the line before. *Adsideo* has the meaning 'to sit as an assessor' in judicial language cf. Tacitus, *Annals* 2.57.4:

> Post quae rarus in tribunali Caesaris Piso, et si quando adsideret, atrox ac dissentire manifestus.

52. *Hybla totos funde flores, quidquid annus adtulit*

totos funde flores. The MSS transmit both *totus* S and *totos* TV. Cameron, in accordance with his assertion that the usage of *totus* as a synonym for *omnis* gives us no information about the Latinity or date of the *Pervigilium* (Cameron 1984: 214), takes the reading of S construing it with *annus* and presumably translating 'the entire year'. As Cameron (*ibid.*) and Catlow (1980: 80) point out, *totus* is an equivalent to *omnis* even in Classical literature (*TLL s.v.*) and confusion over the vowels -*o*- and -*u*- is prevalent in the manuscripts as noted before. (It should be observed that the same confusion has occurred with the word *annus* in MS S which reads *annos* in this line.) With such a scarcity of solid evidence in this situation there only remain subjective preferences for meaning and style for coming to a conclusion about the reading of this line. The preference for the year to produce 'all the flowers' rather than 'the whole year' to produce flowers can be supported by the fact that the whole year does not produce flowers: blossom is limited to the months of spring and summer. Reading *totos* also provides a pause at the diaeresis giving a balance to the line which construing *totus* with *annus* must forsake. While the poet does not choose to make such a pause in every line in the poem by any means, when lines balanced in this way do occur, they usually appear in groups *cf.* lines two and three; twenty-nine to thirty-three; forty-seven and forty-eight; seventy-six to seventy-eight; ninety and ninety-one.

quidquid. The neuter *quidquid* refers back to masculine plural *flores*.

53. *Hybla florum sume vestem quantus Aetnae campus est*

sume vestem. Heinsius proposed *sume vestem* for *superestem* S; *rumpereste* T and *rumpe restem* V in 1665. Convincing palaeographical explanations of the corruption are provided by Clementi (242): the -*te* in T probably derives from the unexpanded abbreviation -*tē*, the *rum*- (TV) from dittography with the end of the previous word *florum* and the -*p*- that appears in all three manuscripts perhaps comes from incorrect expansion of the abbreviation *sūe* for *sume*. The phrase *vestem sumere* is usual in Classical Latin *cf.* Horace, *Satires* 1.2.16 *sumpta veste virili* and Cicero, *De re publica* 1.12.18 *vestimentis sumptis*.

54. *Ruris hic erunt puellae vel puellae montium*

Puellae. Here the term refers to the nymphs as it does in line twenty-nine and more generally in Latin literature *cf.* for example Vergil,

Eclogues 10.9. The *ruris puellae* are perhaps the ἀγρονόμοι νύμφαι of Homer, *Odyssey* 6.105 (Formicola 1998: 154).

vel. The usage of *vel* here is uncommon but the same usage in line ninety (see note below) after the emendation by Thomas (1928), taken up by Bernstein and Newton (2000), confirms the meaning here as 'even'. This can be explained as an intensifying usage which replaces *et* and adds a level of excitement and suspense to the line: 'even the mountain nymphs will be here!'

55. *Quaeque silvas quaeque lucos quaeque fontes incolunt*

fontes. All the manuscripts read *montes*. It was Schriverius who proposed the emendation *fontes*. The reading of the MSS was probably influenced by *montium* in the line above. The first half of the line refers to the Dryads who were the nymphs of the trees and groves while the second half refers to the Naiads, the nymphs of the fountains and streams. Line fifty-four establishes the broad distinction between the country nymphs and the mountain nymphs before going into the more detailed locales that the nymphs inhabit. Note that Sannazarius suggested *fontium* for this line in MS V, presumably for the same reason. For the broad distinction between the types of nymphs *cf.* Homer, *Odyssey* 6.123–4:

> ὥς τέ με κουράων ἀμφήλυθε θῆλυς αὐτή:
> νυμφάων, αἳ ἔχουσ᾽ ὀρέων αἰπεινὰ κάρηνα
> καὶ πηγὰς ποταμῶν καὶ πίσεα ποιήεντα.

lucos. (*locus* S: *locos* T) Confusion of the vowels -*o*- and -*u*- in the MSS is common.

Quaeque . . . quaeque . . . The repetition of the suffix -*que* is suited to the trochaic meter. The poet of the PV has recourse to this same technique in verses twenty-four and sixty-five. For the technique throughout the poem see the note to line one.

56. *Iussit omnes adsidere pueri mater alitis*

pueri. Buecheler emends *pueri* to *dei metri causa,* but as the previous metrical practice of the author has shown (*cf. aleret* line eleven, for example) the fifth foot is not obliged to be filled by a trochee.

alitis. *Ales* is a common epithet for Cupid *cf.* Horace, *Carmina* 2.12.4: *Cythereae puer ales.*

adsidere. There is an element of structural circularity at play in this stanza. *Adsidere* appears both in the second line of the stanza and in this line, the penultimate. Perhaps more striking is the appearance of *iussit* at both the beginning and the end of the stanza. This is a deliberate repetitive mode that we find throughout the poem. It emphasizes here the authoritative character of Venus. See note to line seven.

57. *Iussit et nudo puellas nil Amori credere*

This line brings the reader back to stanza four concerning *Amor* and particularly the second half of line twenty-nine (*puer) nec tamen credi potest.*

credere. An attractive alternative reading for *credere* was proposed in 2006 by Christine Schmitz: she would read *cedere* and translate 'and not to surrender in any way to the God of Love' ('in keiner Weise dem Liebesgott ... nachzugeben') (Schmitz 2006: 363). The reading has obvious verbal parallels in Vergil, *Eclogues* 10.69 (*et nos cedamus Amori*) and, as Schmitz herself argues, it would make for a fittingly strong finish to a stanza in which the dominance of Venus is emphasized, especially in the context of stanza four where Venus – the goddess of reproductive power – is set in opposition to Cupid – a threat to the security of the love celebrated in the festival (Schmitz 2006: 367). The fact that the MSS all agree on the reading *credere,* however, and the use of this verb in connection with Cupid earlier in the poem (stanza four), mean that the grounds for adopting Schmitz's otherwise tempting emendation are less than convincing.

(58). See note on line forty

59. Cras erit quo primus aether copulavit nuptias

The seventh stanza revisits and further develops the theme broached at the start of the poem: the *hieros gamos* of Earth and Sky. The image of the *maritus imber* now extends its role from causing the trees to expose their foliage (line four) to becoming the father of the whole year (line sixty). This stanza emphasizes the primal power of Venus as the goddess of love and the driving force behind creation. As Clementi (1936: 211–12) documents, the passage has Vergilian (*Georgics* 2.325–7) and Lucretian (1.248–53; 2.992–7) echoes. The language of the passage is strikingly Vergilian:

> Tum pater omnipotens fecundis imbribus Aether
> Coniugis in gremium laetae descendit, et omnis
> Magnus alit magno commixtus corpore foetus.
> Avia tum resonant avibus virgulta canoris,
> Et Venerem certis repetunt armenta diebus;
> Parturit almus ager Zephyrique tepentibus auris
> Laxant arva sinus; superat tener omnibus umor,
> Inque novos soles audent se gramina tuto
> credere.
>
> (*Georgics* 2.325–33)

The fragment of Aeschylus's *Danaides* at Athenaeus 13.600b offers a precedent for the underlying idea of the cosmic power of love as a creative force:

> ἐρᾷ μὲν ἁγνὸς οὐρανὸς τρῶσαι χθόνα,
> ἔρως δὲ γαῖαν λαμβάνει γάμου τυχεῖν·
> ὄμβρος δ᾽ ἀπ᾽ εὐνάοντος οὐρανοῦ πεσὼν
> ἔκυσε γαῖαν.

The best treatment of the ideas and the literary tradition that stand behind the *Pervigilium*'s seventh stanza is that of Cucchiarelli's 2003 edition (121–5). The philosophical tone that runs throughout the passage belongs more to the vulgar theoretical milieu of the Classical and Late Antique world. Two terms in particular (the *permeans spiritus* of line sixty-three and the *pervius tenor* in line sixty-six) belong to the Stoic philosophical tradition. See the respective notes on these words below. Important to note, as observed by Cucchiarelli, is the use not only of *Georgics* 2.325–33 above, but also the switch at line sixty-three to another, related Vergilian model: *Aeneid* 6.724–32:

Principio caelum ac terras camposque liquentis
Lucentemque globum lunae Titaniaque astra
spiritus intus alit, totamque infusa per artus
mens agitat molem et magno se corpore miscet.
Inde hominum pecudumque genus vitaeque volantum
Et quae marmoreo fert monstra sub aequore pontus.
Igneus est ollis vigor et caelestis origo
Seminibus, quantum non noxia corpora tardant
Terrinique hebetant artus moribundaque membra.

quo. The MSS *quo* SV; *qui* T was emended to the archaic *quom* by Buecheler (1859). But the poet uses the later form *cum*, upon which all the manuscripts agree, in line ninety-two. And the poem shows very little else in the way of archaisms. The older personal use of *pudebit* on line twenty-six (see note) is known from Plautus but can also be found in the Silver Age poet Lucan. The reading of S and V, *quo*, adopted here, has been defended by Rand (1934b). It stands for 'cras erit tempus quo' or as Schilling suggests 'cras erit dies quo'. Cf. Ovid, *Metamorphoses* 1.256–7 for this type of temporal ablative.

60. *Ut pater totum crearet vernis annum nubibus*

pater. As in the Vergilian model (*Georgics* 2.325), *Aether* is the 'father' in this line.

totum. Accepting Saumaise's emendation from the MSS *totis* gives a more balanced line. The phrase *totus annus* can be found, for example, at Ovid, *Fasti* 1.26 and 168. The sense proposed by Catlow (1980: 83), and followed by Cucchiarelli (2003: 127) adds weight to the emendation: *annus* in this line refers to the yearly cycle of seasons and of growth rather than to the linear, temporal progression of months.

crearet. The indicative *creavit* in S probably stems from an error of *homoioteleuton* with *copulavit* in the line above. Note again the metrical flexibility of the fifth foot with *vernis*, a spondee.

61. *In sinum maritus imber fluxit almae coniugis*

maritus. Following the note to line four, the word *maritus* here can mean both 'husband' as a noun and 'fertile' as an adjective. The two senses of the word are brought out in the corresponding words *coniunx* 'wife' on the one hand, and *alma* 'nurturing' on the other.

62. *Unde foetus mixtus omnis aleret magno corpore*

Unde foetus. For the line in general *cf.* Vergil, *Georgics* 2.326–7: *et omnis/ Magnus alit magno commixtus corpore foetus. Unde* is the reading of MS S against the *ut* of T V. The use of *unde* adds a suggestion of causation to lines sixty-one and sixty-two which is intimated but not explicit in the Vergilian model. For further comparison of the model and the *Pervigilium*'s imitation, see Cucchiarelli (2003: 128).

Aleret is a fifth foot anapaest.

63. *Ipsa venas atque mentem permeanti spiritu*

venas. Vergil, *Aeneid* 4.1–2: *At regina gravi iamdudum saucia cura/ Vulnus alit venis et caeco carpitur igni,* provides a model for the meaning of *venas* found in this line. The *venae* represent the body and emotions, alongside *mens* which stands for the mind and rational thought. For the distinction between the *corpus* and *mens* in philosophical thought, compare Lucretius 4.728–31. Venus rules over all the spheres of the human being as well as holding sway over the rest of the universe. (See line sixty-five.) The division between the rational and the corporeal was already a part of Stoic philosophy and became a common way of viewing the human being in mediaeval literature (Lewis 1964: 156–61; 165–9).

permeanti spiritu. In this line, the *permeans spiritus* had been identified as a translation of the Stoic phrase διήκοντι πνεύματι or τό διῆκον διὰ πάντων πνεῦμα, Galen, *Introductio seu Medicus*, 9 (cited already by Clementi 1936: 217, but also Cucchiarelli 2003: 128). While the phrase is indeed a *terminus technicus* borrowed from Stoic philosophy, the *Pervigilium*'s involvement with ideas of Stocism ought not to be pushed too far. For although the word *spiritus* was used to translate Stoic concepts about the *anima mundi*, the word would also later be used for the Holy Ghost in Christian literature (Abelard equates the *anima mundi* with the *spiritus sanctus*), and the participle *permeans* has been used with *spiritus* in contexts quite outside Stoic philosophy, see for example Apuleius, *De mundo* 25.334 (Catlow 1980: 84). The other phrase more closely associated with Stoicism, *pervius tenor* line sixty-six, also gives a philosophical flavour to this stanza. Verbally, this passage is reminiscent of *Aeneid* 6.724–7:

> Principio caelum et terras camposque liquentes
> Lucentemque globum lunae Titaniaque astra
> Spiritus intus alit, totamque infusa per artus
> Mens agitat molem et magno se corpore miscet

in which Vergil develops a Stoic view of creation. That the philosophical roots of these lines and perhaps the stanza as a whole are Stoic is certain, but it is similarly clear that the blend of other philosophical traditions which appear throughout the piece (*cf.* for example the Epicurean character of line sixty-seven and the twist in the final stanza, at home in the Neo-Platonic tradition) and the isolation of the Stoic influence to this stanza suggest that the poet of the *Pervigilium* intended only to give a philosophical flavour to this part of the poem.

64. *Intus occultis gubernat procreatrix viribus*

Intus. For *intus* with *spiritus cf.* Vergil, *Aeneid* 6.724–7 cited above. See note above for the Stoic implications of the allusion to Vergil.

65. *Perque caelum perque terras perque pontum subditum*

subditum. Following Schilling who translates 'À travers les cieux, à travers les terres, à travers la mer, souveraine' here *subditum* is taken as having been attracted into the singular by *pontum* but referring to the *caelum* and *terras*.

The line is reminiscent of Ovid, *Fasti* 4.93, in context:

> illa quidem totum dignissima temperat orbem,
> illa tenet nullo regna minora deo,
> iuraque dat caelo, terrae, natalibus undis

Note also the use of *illa* in this passage from Ovid, also referring to Venus, as its usage is repeated in the verses following the lines cited and it is similar to the *Pervigilium*'s usage of *ipsa* deferentially referring to the love goddess, see lines forty-one and forty-two for example.

Perque . . . perque. The fondness of the poet for the technique of repeating the -*que* suffix has been remarked upon in the notes to lines one and fifty-five.

66. *Pervium sui tenorem seminali tramite*

Pervium . . . tenorem. The phrase *pervium tenorem* recalls the Stoic idea of ὁ διήκων πνευματικός τόνος (Clement of Alexandria, *Stroma* 5.8.48.2). The τόνος was the force that held the cosmos together in the Stoic conception of the world. For this concept see the *Stoicorum*

Veterum Fragmenta 2.439–62. (Clementi's treatment of this line and its debt to Stoic thinking is very full, see p. 218, as well as Cucchiarelli 2003: 131.) Refer to the notes on line sixty-three for the idea that the use of this technical language is designed to lend an overall 'philosophical' flavour to the passage rather than to present a uniquely Stoic one.

seminalis. A post-classical word.

67. *Imbuit iussitque mundum nosse nascendi vias*

The role of Venus in this line is similar to that of Lucretius, 1.19–20:

omnibus incutiens blandum per pectora amorem
efficis ut cupide generatim saecla propagent.

This Epicurean context attests the author's eclecticism in forming his idea for this 'philosophical' stanza.

68. *Cras amet qui numquam amavit quique amavit cras amet*

The meaning and arrangement of this stanza has emptied many inkpots. The confusion centres on the words *Romuli matrem* (*Romoli matrem* ST, *Romuli matrem* V) in line seventy-four. Solutions have been many and varied. Good accounts of the more convincing attempts at re-arrangement or emendation have been given in Catlow (1980: 87–8), as well as those less convincing in Clementi (1936: 247–51). See below in the comment to line seventy-four for the adoption here of a more recent emendation, which makes the best sense of the line and the stanza as a whole.

Overall, the stanza tells the story of Venus's important role in Rome's history: the journey of the Trojans to Rome, the marriage of Aeneas to Lavinia, the rape of Rhea Silva and the rape of the Sabine women. The stanza closes with the ancestry of the *gens Iulia* up to Caesar.

69. *Ipsa Troianos nepotes in Latinos transtulit*

nepotes. This line commences the short sketch of the involvement of Venus with the history of the Roman people. Rivinus in 1644 proposed that *nepotes* should be replaced by *penates*. The manuscripts read *nepotes* (SV) *nec potes* (T) and while Rivinus's conjecture has considerable poetic merit, the manuscript authority and the sense render the conjecture unnecessary.

70. *Ipsa laurentem puellam coniugem nato dedit*

laurentem puellam. The phrase refers to Aeneas's Italian wife Lavinia. She is given the epithet *laurens* because she was betrothed to Turnus of Laurentum before Aeneas arrived in Italy. Turnus is found with the same epithet at *Aeneid* 7.650. The emphasis on the role of Venus can be understood by reference to book seven of the *Aeneid*, where the narrative deals with Juno's opposition to the proposed marriage between Lavinia and Aeneas. The anger of Juno, her summoning of the fury Allecto and her influence on both Amata, wife of King Latinus, and Turnus himself, was in response to the anticipated marriage of Aeneas and Lavinia supported by Venus.

71. *Moxque Marti de sacello dat pudicam virginem*

dat pudicam virginem. The line refers to the rape of Rhea Silvia, a Vestal virgin, by Mars (Livy, 1.3–4). This union bore the twins Romulus and Remus. The verb *dare* often can mean 'to give in marriage' (*cf. ei filiam suam in matrimonium dat*, Caesar, *Bellum Gallicum* 1.3.5) and so this phrase hides, along with *pudicam virginem*, the real character of the encounter. This is part of the poet's characterization of Venus as the goddess of upstanding relations and marriage, as well as being euphemistic. The virtuous treatment of Venus's role in love affairs has been noted on line seven and is evident in the poet's focus on marriage at the end of his virgin/rose stanza '*unico marita nodo non pudebit* *solvere*' (twenty-six) diverging from the traditional end of similar comparisons between the blossom of the rose and maidenhood. (See note on line twenty-six.)

72. *Romuleas ipsa fecit cum Sabinis nuptias*

Romuleas. The MSS *Romuleas* SV; *Rumuleas* T has triggered emendations among previous editors: *Romulares* (Rigler), *Romulas et* (Statius) or *Romulaeas* (Pithou) for example. The root of the problem lies in the scansion of *Romulĕus* at Ovid, *Fasti* 3.67 and Vergil, *Aeneid* 8.654, for example, where the usual rule applies *vocalis ante vocalem corripitur* (Raven 1965: 24): when two vowels occur together and do not form a diphthong the former vowel is short. The vowel *e* would need to be long here. However, the quantity of syllables in proper names were somewhat flexible in the poets. Compare, for example Catullus, 64.37, where the poet has *Pharsăliam coeunt, Pharsālia tecta frequentant* in the same line. In another, closer parallel *Daedaleus* is scanned *Daedalĕum (iter)* at Propertius, 2.14.8 while at Horace, *Carmina* 4.2.2 it appears *(ope) Daedalēa.*

fecit . . . nuptias. The phrase *nuptias facere* can be found as early as Plautus, *Aulularia* 2.2.83. This is a similar disguising of events as found in the previous line. However, the phrasing here does follow the result of the episode in Livy, 1.9.3: *Sed ipse Romulus circumibat docebatque . . . illas tamen in matrimonio . . . fore.*

73. *Unde Ramnes et Quirites proque prole posterum*

Ramnes et Quirites. At Livy, 1.13.8 and Propertius, 4.1.31 a third ancient Italian tribe, the *Luceres* is mentioned. Schilling (1944: 24) explains the appearance in the *Pervigilium* of only two of the tribes: in the first place the *Luceres* were outside of the marriage bond approved by Venus. Secondly that the Roman story has always focused on the two tribes, the *Ramnes* (the Roman element) and the *Quirites* (the

Sabine), perhaps, as Catlow adds, because including the *Luceres* would acknowledge an Etruscan presence in the Roman blood-line.

74. *Iulium mater crearet et nepotem Caesarem*

Iulium mater. The MSS offer *Romoli* ST; *Romuli* V and *matrem* STV. In this form the phrase *Romuli mater* MSS would most easily refer to Rhea Silvia (Ilia) who already appears on line seventy-one. Such wording introduces a good deal of chronological and mythological confusion into the passage. The meaning that would make the most sense in the stanza would be for line seventy-four to refer to the Julian line, Augustus Caesar and his offspring. The *gens Iulia* traced their ancestry back to Aeneas and his mother Venus – as alluded to already in lines sixty-nine and seventy. (See Suetonius, *Life of Caesar* 6 and Ennius, *Annales* 53 for this well-known claim.) A convincing emendation along these very lines has been offered by P. S. Davies (1992). He proposes *Iulium mater* (though see Bury (1905: 304) for *mater*). As a palaeographical explanation, Davies suggests that the error occurred as the result of a copyist's eye slipping up to line seventy-two (perhaps helped along by Ramnes in line seventy-three) and copying *Rom-* instead of the correct word. Davies (1992: 576) provides a plausible but convoluted description of how the error may then have resulted in the form *Romuli*. A more simple account of the corruption might be that the scribe began the line writing *Rom-* from line seventy-two, but then taking his eyes from the page again completed the word with *iulium*. Throughout the later copying process the initial *i-* was then swallowed into the minim group of the letter *-m-* and the final *-m* was omitted by haplograpy with the initial *m-* of *mater*. The simple 'correction' was then made from the remaining **Romuliu* to *Romuli*. From a stylistic point of view Davies' emendation restores the balance in the line since *Iulium* is arranged so as to complement both *nepotem* and *Caesarem*.

nepotem. *Nepos* has its broader poetical meaning here as 'descendant'. *Cf. in nepotum Perniciem,* Horace, *Carmina* 2.13.3: *Caesar, ab Aenea qui tibi fratre nepos,* Ovid, *Epistolae ex Ponto* 3.3.62: *magnanimos Remi nepotes,* Catullus, 68.5

76. Rura fecundat voluptas, rura Venerem sentiunt

Rura. This stanza brings the reader back to the rural scene that was imagined at the start of the poem. Venus is imagined here in her older guise as a fertility goddess before she was brought into line with the Greek Aphrodite (Clementi 1936: 256).

Venerem. The stanza depicts another side of Venus's character after she is described as the *genetrix* of the cosmos in stanza seven and then as *genetrix* of the Roman people in stanza eight. Cupid is also brought back into the scene in a different guise; he is not envisaged with any of the mischievousness that he had in stanza four and remains simply the *puer Dionae rure natus* in this penultimate section of the poem. The transition back to the natural setting sets the scene for the very different tone of the final stanza.

Venerem sentiunt. Note the anapaestic sixth foot in this line. For examples of the phrase *Venerem sentire* see Nemesianus, *Eclogues* 4.27 and Seneca, *Phaedra* 567.

77. Ipse Amor, puer Dionae, rure natus dicitur

puer . . . rure natus. This setting for the birth of *Amor* can be found in Tibullus, 2.1.67:

> Ipse interque greges interque armenta Cupido
> Natus, et indomitas dicitur inter equas.

78. Hunc ager cum parturiret, ipsa suscepit sinu

Hunc ager cum parturiret. Two interpretations of this line have been commonly adopted by commentators. The first, argued in full by

Clementi (1936: 257), proposes taking *ager cum parturiret* as a phrase equivalent to *verno tempore*. He thus reads: *Hunc, ager cum parturiret, ipsa suscepit sinu*. *Parturiret* can be found with this intransitive meaning at Vergil, *Georgics* 2.330, lines which should also be compared for language and imagery. A second approach takes the lines as: *hunc ager cum parturiret, ipsa suscepit sinu*, adopted by earlier editors Pithou (1587) and Buecheler (1859). In this reading, *hunc* is the object of the fields' labour. The fact that the previous line has Cupid expressly as the son of Venus *puer Dionae* does not rule out the inclusion of another tradition for his birth (Cucchiarelli 2003: 139). The natural rhythm of the line, with a pause at the diaeresis after *parturiret*, suggests that this is the correct way to take the phrase. Indeed, the metrical division of the line speaks against Lipsius's otherwise attractive third alternative: *hunc ager, cum parturiret ipsa, suscepit sinu* (1580), which has the benefit of preserving the standard mythological story that Amor is Venus's son.

79. *Ipsa florum delicatis educavit osculis*

educavit osculis. This line brings the reader back to line twenty-three, where *Amor* is said to have made roses from his kisses. *Educare* has the meaning here of both physical and spiritual upbringing: Cupid was raised among the flowers. For the close association between Love and flowers compare Plato, *Symposium* 196a–b:

χρόας δὲ κάλλος ἡ κατ' ἄνθη δίαιτα τοῦ θεοῦ σημαίνει· ἀνανθεῖ γὰρ καὶ ἀπηνθηκότι καὶ σώματι καὶ ψυχῇ καὶ ἄλλῳ ὁτῳοῦν οὐκ ἐνίζει Ἔρως, οὗ δ' ἂν εὐανθής τε καὶ εὐώδης τόπος ᾖ, ἐνταῦθα δὲ καὶ ἵζει καὶ μένει.

81. *Ecce iam subter genestas explicant tauri latus*

subter. For *subter* all the manuscripts read *super*, but the idea that the bulls were stretched out on top of the broom bush is strange especially when it seems to be providing shade for the flocks in line eighty-three.

Broukhusius in 1708 saw that *subter* was the correct reading. *Subter* was often written *supter* presumably after the labial plosive became unvoiced in assimilating with the voiceless dental that follows it. *Supter* could then be easily corrupted to *super*. Broukhusius cited the similar image at Calpurnius Siculus, 1.1.4–5 in support of his emendation, which has been cited frequently by later editors:

> Cernis ut, ecce, pater quas tradidit, Ornyte, vaccae
> Molle sub hirsuta latus explicuere genesta.

Further evidence that *genestae* were indeed of sufficient size to provide shade for cattle can be found at Vergil, *Georgics* 2.434.

Tauri. Scaliger's correction of the MSS *aonii* seems certain. The error was convincingly explained by Valgiglio who proposed that the initial *t-* was omitted through haplography in the first place. Scaliger's emendation trumps those of Lipsius (*agni*) and Baehrens (*apri*) on account of the sense. Lambs are unlikely to be involved with a *coniugale foedus* and boars would be out of place in the scene of pastoral and herd animals.

82. *Quisque tutus quo tenetur coniugali foedere*

Tutus. The word represents the security of the love which the poet imagines Venus to inspire in the *Pervigilium* and which has been a theme throughout the piece, see note on line seventy-one for example. MS S transmits *tutus* while TV reads *tuus*. Given the very adequate and fitting sense of *tutus* in the line, as well as within the context of the poem at large, there is no need for the *laetus* adopted first by Prasch in 1666, or the *torvus* of Baehrens.

83. *Subter umbras cum maritis ecce balantum greges*

maritis. The emphasis on marriage throughout the poem is carried through to the animals in this final stanza, although this is known from the classical tradition: see Horace, *Carmina* 1.17.7.

balantum greges. This phrase too is well attested in the Classical authors:

> Balantumque gregem fluvio mersare salubri
>
> (Vergil, *Georgics* 1.272)

and also *Aeneid* 7.538. Indeed, the participle has an even longer history as the sound of the flocks, *cf.* Ennius, *Annales* 186.

84. *Et canoras non tacere Diva iussit alites*

canoras . . . alites. This phrase refers back to the idea in line two: *ver canorum*. Birds are unsurprisingly described as *canorus* throughout Latin poetry: *cf.* Horace, *Carmina* 2.20.25–6, for example, and among late antique authors Tiberianus, significantly, uses the image at *Amnis Ibat* 15–16. However, an extra dimension is added to the description of the sound of the birds here in the *Pervigilium* where it is distinguished from the musically uninformative *balantum* in the line above (Formicola 1998: 177).

85. *Iam loquaces ore rauco stagna cygni perstrepunt*

cygni. The introduction of the swan into the scene here begins the transition into the minor key which will characterize the last eight lines of the poem. The song of the swan is known from antiquity to be a forewarning of its own death (see Ovid, *Metamorphoses* 14.428–30). However, the poet is still singing in the positive tone in this line. The atmospheric tension here perhaps foreshadows that which will follow at the poem's 'turn' in line eighty-nine. The swan is associated with Venus and pictured pulling her chariot (see Ovid, *Metamorphoses* 10.713; Horace, *Carmina* 4.1.10) and at Statius, *Silvae* 1.2.145–6:

> Pandit nitidos domus alta penates
> Claraque gaudentes plauserunt limina cygni

The line as a whole is indebted both verbally and conceptually to Vergil, *Aeneid* 11.458: *dant sonitum rauci per stagna loquacia cygni.*

86. *Adsonat Terei puella subter umbram populi*

Terei puella. The sad myth of Tereus, Philomela and Procne is invoked in the next five lines. Only Tereus's name is mentioned specifically while the nightingale is alluded to in lines eighty-six to eighty-eight and in line ninety the *chelidon*, a Graecism (χελιδών), for the Latin *hirundo* 'a swallow', appears named unequivocally. This current line certainly refers to the nightingale because in any version of the myth it is the nightingale which flies into the trees, whereas the swallow flies to the roof of the house cf. Ovid, *Metamorphoses* 6.412–676; Catullus, 65.11–15 and Vergil, *Georgics* 4.511–12:

> Qualis populea maerens Philomela sub umbra
> Amissos queritur fetus

Indeed, the similarity of the image (*umbra populi*) and the language (*queror* line eighty-eight) suggests that Vergil's lines were the model for the *Pervigilium*'s rendition of the theme. The nightingale's song is imagined as a song of lament in the classical tradition, see lines quoted above and Ovid, *Heroides* 15.135–6 for example. The despondent character of the nightingale's song corresponds with the symbolism of the song of the *Terei puella* in this stanza: *queri* (line eighty-eight).

All three main characters in the myth are present in some form. Tereus is only mentioned in passing and the nightingale is simply alluded to for its beautiful (*ore musico* line eighty-seven) yet sad song. It seems of little consequence for the poem to identify exactly which mythological sister was which bird in the poet's mind for he makes it very clear which bird is the most significant later in the *Pervigilium* by naming it clearly: *Quando fiam vel chelidon . . .* (line ninety). In fact the classical tradition itself even interchanged the names of the birds so that in Ovid's account it is Procne who is the wife of Tereus and who becomes the swallow and Philomela the violated sister who becomes the nightingale. In *Georgics* 4.511–12, however, Philomela is the wife and mourns the child she killed in revenge. Ovid's more popular account of the story was the one that was taken up by mediaeval and modern authors (Chandler 1934: 79).

The internal evidence of the poem suggests that for the *Pervigilium* author, Philomela was the wife of Tereus, and mother of the child Itys whom she killed. Previous editors have gathered together the evidence that *puella* can take the meaning 'young bride': Ovid, *Heroides* 1.115; 4.2 (cited by Clementi 1936: 261) and Propertius, 4.3.72 (cited by Schilling 1944) for example, which makes the nightingale (*Terei puella*) 'the young wife of Tereus'.

87. Ut putes motus amoris ore dici musico

motus amoris. The combination *motus amoris* has only one precedent in Cicero, *Laelius de Amicitia* 9.29, but the word *motus* is commonly used with a genitive noun to indicate a state of mind *cf. cum semper agitetur animus, nec principium motus habeat*, Cicero, *Post Reditum in Senatu* 21.78; *De Officiis* 1.36.130.

putes. The technique of appealing to the reader towards the end of the poem by using the colloquial *putes* is also found in line fifteen of Tiberianus's *Amnis Ibat* (see authorship and date discussion as well as appendix for further context):

> Has per umbras omnis ales plus canora quam *putes*
> Cantibus vernis strepebat et susurris dulcibus

88. Et neges queri sororem de marito barbaro

Three contending readings have been proposed for this line where the trouble centres on the interpretation of the word *soror*. Schilling (1944: 28) suggests in a short note on the line that the *sororem* is the object of *queri*. He then translates: 'on ne dirait pas qu'elle (the nightingale) plaint une sœur, victime de son barbare époux'. Although not impossible, this is an awkward way to take the Latin. Moreover, the nightingale is imagined throughout the Classical tradition to sing a song of individual grief as a mother for her dead child and not for the other characters in the myth as Schilling would have her do here. Catlow (1980: 95–6) proposes reading the Latin in the natural manner with the *sororem* as the accusative subject of the infinitive *queri*. However, he would have *soror* refer to the sister of the nightingale and paraphrases: 'you would think that she sang the emotions of love; you would deny that her sister (the swallow) was lamenting a brutal lover'. But in the mythological tradition the swallow's singing is presented as an ambiguous song hailing the coming of spring and all the uncertainty which that season brings with it. Moreover, the verb *queror* and its cognates are connected with the song of the nightingale repeatedly in the ancient authors, see the passage quoted from the *Georgics* above (upon which the present passage may be modelled) and in Seneca's *Octavia* (914–16) where the eponymous character laments her suffering at the hands of Nero:

> quis mea digne deflere potest
> mala? quae lacrimis nostris questus
> reddere aëdon?

Rand (1934b) proposed taking *sororem* as the accusative subject of *queri*; however, he has *soror* refer to the *Terei puella* of line eighty-six, i.e. the nightingale. This reading is the strongest because it maintains the association of the song of lament with the nightingale in accordance with the literary tradition. It also keeps the nightingale's lament personal and directed at her own brutal husband. Furthermore, the obvious parallelism of the pair of lines (eighty-seven and eighty-eight) is not disrupted by a change of subject as it is in the case of the alternative proposals.

The major objection to Rand's reading is that the word *soror* is redundant in this line if it only refers again to the nightingale. However, the poet, who has so far only alluded to the myth of Procne, Philomela and

Tereus by using the name of only one character (*Terei*) and alluding to the song of the nightingale (*ore musico*), here further indicates that he is indeed referring to the myth of the daughters of Pandion by making the nightingale a sister, as she is in the story. This subtly signals to the reader the coming reference to the swallow in the following verses.

The *chelidon* is the only bird in the myth specified by name in the *Pervigilium*. This demonstrates the emphatic effect that the poet wishes to achieve in line ninety. The emphasis on the swallow and the direct comparison of the poet to the bird is further amplified if the reader is already anticipating the appearance of the myth's final character. By referring to the nightingale as a sister in this line the poet tells the reader to expect the arrival of the *chelidon*, an expectation which is satisfyingly fulfilled in line ninety.

marito barbaro. The *maritus barbarus* is Tereus who violated his wife's sister and cut out her tongue to prevent her from revealing his crime. Ovid used this vocabulary in connection with Tereus's deeds in his account of the story at *Metamorphoses* 6.533.

89. *Illa cantat; nos tacemus. Quando ver venit meum?*

Illa. In accordance with the note on the line above, *Illa* in this line refers to the nightingale. The extreme and severe contrast between the beautiful song of the nightingale and the author's silence is neatly encapsulated in the opposition of *Illa cantat; nos tacemus*. This acute disparity between the author's opinion of his own song and that of the nightingale explains the reason that he sets his sights lower in the next line and wishes only to be like the less tuneful and ambiguous swallow. The contrast between the swallow and nightingale is suggested too in this line. In using the pronoun *Illa* 'that woman', the reader might be prompted to imagine a contrast with *haec* 'this woman' or perhaps *ista* (although the negative connotations of *iste* would not be appropriate here). The *haec*, 'the lady closer by', both literally (she appears on the next line) and in terms of sense (the poet compares himself directly with her), is the *chelidon*.

90. *Quando fiam vel chelidon ut tacere desinam?*

Quando fiam vel chelidon. The manuscripts transmit: *Quando fiam* (S) / *faciam* (TV) *ut* (STV) *chelidon* … These readings introduce a hiatus into the line which is not metrically acceptable. Rivinus made the economical emendation of the first *ut* to *uti* which solves the metrical problem but introduces the awkward use of *uti* and *ut* in the same line. Some editors, recently Cameron and Cucchiarelli for example, have taken the *faciam* of TV. This introduces a tribrach into the second foot which, although permissible, does not occur elsewhere in the poem. The distant possibility of poet transforming into a swallow, signalled by the use of *vel* here, 'introducing what might be thought an extreme or unlikely possibility' (*s.v.* OLD), supports the reading of S with the passive *fiam*.

In 2000 Neil Bernstein and Francis Newton took up the older suggestion of P. Thomas (1928: 1065–6) that *ut* might be emended to *vel*. The modern scholars do not show any knowledge of Thomas's much earlier proposal. On palaeographical grounds the conjecture is strong: they propose that the common abbreviation of *vel* to *uł* was responsible for the corruption in a common ancestor of the surviving manuscripts. The confusion, well-known to students of Latin palaeography (Havet 1911: h.772) was perhaps helped along by the tendency, demonstrated in places by the oldest surviving manuscript S, of occasionally changing from a majuscule hand (uncial in the case of S) to minuscule lettering (Bernstein, Newton 2000: 328). The conjecture removes the hiatus and unravels the meaning of the poet's anguished appeal in the final stanza. The poet, far from thinking himself worthy of comparison with the nightingale, a bird celebrated for its sad but beautiful song often aligned with elegiac poetry (Rosati 1996: 214–15), wishes merely to become the *chelidon*, the swallow, whose reputation is far lowlier: the swallow is known in the Greek and Latin tradition for its chattering song, see for example Vergil, *Georgics* 9.307: *garrula hirundo*. For the extended analysis of this line, and its implications for the meaning of the poem, see the interpretation of the final stanza and the poem in the introduction.

91. *Perdidi musam tacendo, nec me Phoebus respicit.*

Phoebus. Apollo, described on line forty-six of the poem as the *poetarum deus*, appears here again connected with song, his principle significance in the poem. The poet explains in part the cause of his pain in the final stanza: *perdidit musam*.

respicit. The word *respicio* is commonly used with gods to mean 'take notice of, be mindful of' *cf.* for example Cicero, *Epistolae ad Atticum* 1.16.6, *nisi quis nos deus respexerit*.

92. *Sic Amyclas, cum tacerent, perdidit silentium*

Amyclas. Clementi (1936: 263–9) has vast notes on this town and its silence. The proverbial silence of the town is noted by Erasmus in his *Adagia* (*AC* 809) and appears in the Latin tradition notably at Vergil, *Aeneid* 10.564.

93. *Cras amet qui numquam amavit quique amavit cras amet*

The inclusion of this final refrain is a 'masterstroke of irony' (Rand 1934a). It underlines the poet's melancholy and connects the final stanza, which is separate from the previous eighty lines of the piece in tone and voice, to the rest of the poem. This sense of irony and displacement goes some way to explaining the poet's choice of setting for his poem, which concludes on a personal and sorrowful note, at a rural festival of Venus: the poet feels disconnected from the more general joyous feelings of spring and from the rest of the world, he is isolated from the scene he has created by his lack of song.

Bibliography

AC: Erasmus, D. *Adagiorum chiliades tres, ac centuriae fere totidem*. Basle: J. Froben, 1517.

Agozzino, T. 'Una preghiera gnostica pagana e lo stile lucreziano del IV secolo'. In: *Dignam Dis a Giampaolo Vallot (1934–1966)*, edited by the Istituto di Filologia latina dell' Università di Padova, 169–210. Venice: Libreria Universitaria Editrice, 1972.

AL: Shackleton Bailey, D. R. *Anthologia Latina I*. Stuttgart: Bibliotheca Teubneriana, 1982.

Albertson, L. L. 'Pervigilium Veneris und Nachtfeier der Venus. G. A. Bürgers Liedstil und sein lateinisches Vorbild'. *Arcadia: Internationale Zeitschrift für Literaturwissenschaft* 16, no. 1–3 (2009): 1–12.

Allen, W. S. *Vox Latina*. Cambridge: Cambridge University Press, 1970.

Axt, C. A. M. – See Rigler.

Baehrens, A. *Poetae Latini Minores IV*. Leipzig: Teubner, 1882.

Balde, J. *Poemata*. 4 vols, vol. 4. Cologne: Busaeus, 1660.

Balde, J. 'Philomela'. In: *Jacobi Baldi Opera poetica Omnia*. Edited by M. Happach and F. X. Schlütter, 8 vols, 8: 249–50. Munich: Typis Joannis Lucae Straubii, 1729.

Balde, J. *Opera poetica omnia*. Neudruck der Ausgabe München 1729. Edited with introduction by W. Kühlmann and H. Wiegand. 8 vols, vol. 8. Frankfurt am Main: Keip, 1990.

Bergk, T. *Commentatio de Pervigilium Veneris*. Halle: Hendeliis, 1859.

Bernstein, N. and F. Newton. 'The Text of Pervigilium Veneris 90: A Proposed Emendation'. *The Classical Quarterly* 50, no. 1 (2000): 327–9.

Bischoff, B. 'Panorama der Handschriftenüberlieferung aus der Zeit Karls des Grossen'. In: *Karl der Grosse: Lebenswerk und Nachleben*, edited by W. Braunfels and H. Beumann. 5 vols, 2: 233–54. Düsseldorf: L. Schwann, 1965.

Blänsdorf, J. *Fragmenta Poetarum Latinorum Epicorum et Lyricorum*.[4] Berlin, New York: De Gruyter, 2011.

Bonfante, L. and J. L. Sebasta. *The World of Roman Costume*. Madison: University of Wisconsin Press, 1994.

Bonnefons, J. *Pancharis*. Paris: Ex officina Abelis l'Angelier, 1587.

Booth, A. *The Waste Land from the Bottom Up*. Basingstoke: Palgrave Macmillan, 2015.

Bouhier, J. 'Lettres . . . au R. P. Oudin contenant des remarques sur le Pervigilium Veneris'. *Nouvelles littéraires* 11 (1720): 366–92.

Boyancé, P. 'Encore le Pervigilium Veneris'. *Revue des études latines* 28 (1950): 212–35.

Boyancé, Pierre. 'Le "Pervigilium Veneris" et les "veneralia"'. *Publications de l'école française de Rome* 11, no. 1 (1972): 383–99.

Brakman, C. 'Quando Pervigilium Veneris conditum est?' *Mnemosyne* 56 (1928): 254–70.

Broukhusius, J. *Albii Tibulli, equitis Romani, quae exstant, ad fidem veterum membranarum sedulo castigata: accedunt notae, cum Variar. Lectionum Libello, et terni Indices; quorum primus Omnes Voces Tibullianas complectitur*. Amsterdam: Officina Wetsteniana, 1708: Amstelaedami, ex officina Wetsteniana.

Buecheler, F. *Pervigilium Veneris*. Leipzig: Teubner, 1859.

Buecheler, F. and A. Riese. *Anthologia Latina, sive Poesis latinae supplementum*. 3 vols, vol. 2, 2nd edn. Leipzig: Teubner, 1906.

Bürger, G. A. 'Rechenschaft über die Veränderungen in der Nacht Feier der Venus'. In: *Gottfried August Bürgers sämtliche Schriften*, edited by K. Reinhard. 4 vols, 4: 471–596. Göttingen: H. Dieterich, 1796–1802.

Bury, J. B. 'On the Pervigilium Veneris'. *The Classical Review* 19 (1905): 304.

Cameron, A. 'The Pervigilium Veneris'. *La poesia tardoantica: tra retorica, teologia e politica*. Atti del V Corso della Scuola Superiore di Archeologia e Civiltà Medievali, Messina: Università degli studi di Messina, Centro di studi umanistici (1984): 209–34.

Capponi, F. P. *Ovidii Nasonis Halieuticon Volume I – Introduzione e Testo*. 2 vols, vol. 1. Leiden: E. J. Brill, 1972.

Catlow, L. 'Pervigilium Veneris'. *Latomus revue d'études latines* 172. Brussels: Latomus (1980).

Cazzaniga, I. 'Saggio critico ed esegetico sul Pervigilium Veneris'. *Studi classici e orientali* 3 (1955): 46–101.

Cazzaniga, I. *Carmina Ludicra Romanorum: Pervigilium – Priapea*. Turin: G. B. Paravia, 1959.

Chandler, A. R. 'The Nightingale in Greek and Latin Poetry'. *The Classical Journal* 30, no. 2 (1934): 78–84.

Clarke, W. M. 'Intentional Rhyme in Vergil and Ovid'. *Transactions and Proceedings of the American Philological Association* 103 (1972): 49–77.

Clementi, C. *Pervigilium Veneris, The Vigil of Venus Edited with Facsimiles of the Codex Salmasianus, Codex Thuaneus and Codex Sannazarii: An Introduction, Translation, Apparatus Criticus, Bibliography and Explanatory Notes*. 3rd edn. Oxford: Blackwell and Mott Ltd, 1936.

Clover, F. M. 'Felix Karthago'. *Dumbarton Oaks Papers* 40 (1986): 1–16

Condoñer, C. 'On the One and the Diverse: Pervigilium Veneris'. In: *New Perspectives on Late Antiquity*, edited by D. Hernández de la Fuente, 263–87. Newcastle: Cambridge Scholars Publishing, 2011.

Courtney, E. 'Pervigilium Veneris 35'. *The Classical Journal* 100, no. 4 (2005): 401–02.

Croft, P. J. *The Poems of Robert Sidney. Edited from the Poet's Autograph Notebook*. Oxford: Clarendon Press, 1984.

Crusius, C. *Probabilia critica in quibus veteres graeci latinique scriptores emendantur et declarantur*. Leipzig: Fritschius, 1738: 271–2.

Cucchiarelli, A. *La Veglia di Venere. Pervigilium Veneris: Introduzione, traduzione e note*. Milan: Biblioteca Universale Rizzoli, 2003.

Currie, H. MacL. 'Pervigilium Veneris'. *Aufstieg und Niedergang der römischen Welt* II, 34, 1: 207–24. Berlin, New York: Walter de Gruyter, 1993.

Davies, P. S. 'The Text of Pervigilium Veneris 74'. *The Classical Quarterly* 42, no. 2 (1992): 575–7.

Dousa, J. (The Younger). *Coniectanea in Catullum, Tibullum, Propertium*. Leiden Officina Plantiniana, apud Franciscum Raphelengium, 1588.

Duff, J. W. and A. M. Duff. *Minor Latin Poets*. London: William Heinemann, 1935.

Durant, G. *Imitations tirées du Latin de Jean Bonnefons, avec autres amours et meslanges poétiques, de l'invention de l'Autheur*. Paris: L'Angelier, 1588.

Elsie, R. 'The Hybrid Soil of the Balkans: A Topography of Albanian Literature'. In: *History of the Literary Cultures of East–Central Europe: Junctures and Disjunctions in the 19th and 20th centuries*, edited by

Marcel Cornis-Pope and John Neubauer. 4 vols, 2: 283–301. Amsterdam, Philadelphia: John Benjamins Publishing, 2006.

Erasmus of Rotterdam – see *AL*.

Formicola, C. *Pervigilium Veneris*. Naples: Loffredo Editore, 1998.

Fort, J. A. *The Pervigilium Veneris in Quatrains*. London; Oxford: Humphrey Milford; Oxford University Press, 1922.

Fraenkel, E. 'Die Vorgeschichte des versus quadratus'. *Hermes* 62, no. 3 (1927): 357–70.

Gruter, J. [Rhanutius Gherus] *Delitiae Poetarum Gallorum*. Frankfurt am Main: J. Rosa, 1609.

Havet, L. *Manuel de Critique Verbal Appliquée aux Textes Latins*. Edizione Anastatica ed. Roma: L'erma di Bretschneider, 1911.

Heikkinen, S. 'The Resurrection and Afterlife of an Archaic Metre: Bede, the Carolingians and the Trochaic Septenarius'. *Classica et Mediaevalia* 65 (2016): 241–81.

Hermann, L. 'Claudius Antonius et le Pervigilium Veneris'. *Latomus revue d'études latines* 12. Brussels: Latomus (1953): 53–69.

HLL – see Smolak.

[Jones, W.] *Poems consisting chiefly of translations from the Asiatick languages: To which are added two essays, I. On the poetry of the Eastern nations. II. On the arts, commonly called imitative*. Oxford: Clarendon Press, 1772.

Jones, W. *Poeseos Asiaticae commentariorum libri sex: cum appendice; subjicitur Limon, seu miscellaneorum liber*. London: T. Cadell, 1774.

[Jones, W.] *Poems consisting chiefly of translations from the Asiatick languages: To which are added two essays, I. On the poetry of the Eastern nations. II. On the arts, commonly called imitative*. 2nd edn. London: N. Conant, 1777.

Kahl, P., ed. *Das Bundesbuch des Göttinger Hains: Edition-historische Untersuchung-Kommentar*. Tübingen: Walter de Gruyter, 2006.

Kelliher, H. and K. Duncan-Jones. 'A Manuscript of Poems by Robert Sidney: Some Early Impressions'. *The British Library Journal* 1, no. 2 (1975): 107–44.

Kühlmann, W. and H. Wiegand, eds. *Jacob Balde SJ: Opera poetica omnia*. Reprint of the 1729 Munich Edition with Text and Introduction. 8 vols, vol. 8. Frankfurt am Main: Keip, 1990.

[L. D. P.] *Traduction en prose et en vers d'une ancienne hymne sur les fêtes de Vénus, intitulée Pervigilium Veneris.* London and Paris: Barbou, 1766.

Lemaire, N. E. *Poetae Latini Minores.* Paris: Lemaire, 1824.

Lewis, C. S. *The Discarded Image.* Cambridge: Cambridge University Press, 1964.

Lewy, H. 'A Latin Hymn to the Creator Ascribed to Plato'. *The Harvard Theological Review* 39, no. 4 (1946): 243–58.

Lipsius, I. *Electorum liber I.* Antwerp: Christophorus Plantinus, 1580.

Ludwig, W. 'Giovanni Pontano und das *Pervigilium Veneris* des Jean Bonnefons'. *Neulateinisches Jahrbuch* 4 (2002): 197–213.

Mackail, J. W. *Catullus, Tibullus, Pervigilium Veneris.* Cambridge, Massachusetts; London: Harvard University Press; William Heinemann, 1913.

Martin, G. 'Transposition of Verses in the Pervigilium Veneris'. *Classical Philology* 30, no. 3 (1935): 255–59.

Mattiacci, S. *I carmi e i frammenti di Tiberiano: Introduzione, edizione critica, traduzione e commento.* Florence: Leo S. Olschki editore, 1990.

Mommsen, T. *C. Iulii Solini Collectanea Rerum Memorabilium.* Berlin: Weidmann, 1895.

Noel, F. *Traduction complète des Poésies de Catulle, suivie des Poésies de Gallus et de la Veillée des Fêtes de Vénus.* Paris: Crapelet, 1803.

Norberg, D. *Introduction à l'Étude de la Versification Latine Médiévale.* Stockholm: Almqvist and Wiksell, 1958.

Omont, H. 'Sur le Pervigilium Veneris, I. Conjectures de Joseph Scaliger'. *Revue de Philologie* 9 (1885): 124–6.

Orelli, J. C. *Phaedri Aug. Liberti Fabulae Aesopiae : prima editio critica cum Integra varietate codd. Pithoeani, Remensis, Danielini, Perottini, et editionis principis, reliqua vero selecta: accedunt Caesaris Germanici Aratea ex fide codd. Basil. Bern. Einsiedl. Freiberg, ed. principis emendata et suppleta : Pervigilium Veneris ad codd. Salmas. et Pith, exactum.* Zurich: Orelli and Fuesslini, 1831.

Owen, S. G. *Catullus with the Pervigilium Veneris.* London: Lawrence and Bullen, 1893.

Pagés, G. H. 'Rosas y perlas en el *Pervigilium Veneris*'. *Anales de Filología Clásica* 6 (1954): 197–205.

Pagés, G. H. 'Sobre la datación del *Pervigilium Veneris*.' *Anales de Filología Clásica* 11 (1986): 105–17.

Palmer, L. R. *The Latin Language*. 4th edn. London: Faber and Faber Ltd, 1954.

Parnell, T. *Poems on several occasions: Written by Dr. Thomas Parnell, . . . and published by Mr. Pope*. Edited by A. Pope. London: printed for B. Lintot, 1721.

Pascal, P. 'The Conclusion of the Pervigilium Veneris.' *Neophilologus* 49 (1965): 1–5.

Perini, G. B. 'Per la datazione del Pervigilium Veneris.' *Storia, letteratura e arte a Roma nel secondo secolo dopo Cristo. Atti del Convegno: Mantova 8–10 ottobre 1992* (1995): 139–58.

Perono Cacciafoco, F. 'Sincretismo filosofico–religioso e tradizione nell'inno al *Deus Omnipotens* di Tiberiano.' *Atene e Roma* (2nd new series) 4, no. 1–2 (2012): 90–110.

Prasch, J. L. *Poematum libellus: accedit Pervigilium Veneris, innominati poetae opus, emendatuni et notis auctum*. Nuremberg: W. E. Felseckerus, 1666.

Raby, F. J. E. *A History of Secular Latin Poetry in the Middle Ages*. 2 vols, vol. 2. Oxford: Clarendon Press, 1957.

Rand, E. K. 'Spirit and Plan of the Pervigilium Veneris.' *Transactions and Proceedings of the American Philological Association* 65 (1934a): 1–12.

Rand, E. K. 'Sur le Pervigilium Veneris.' *Revue des études latines* 12 (1934b): 83–95.

Rand, E. K. Review: 'Pervigilium Veneris by C. Clementi.' *The American Journal of Philology* 58, no. 4 (1937): 474–8.

Raven, D. S. *Latin Metre: An Introduction*. London: Faber and Faber, 1965.

Riese, A. *Anthologia Latina I, Libri Salmasiani aliorumque carmina*, 2nd edn. Leipzig: Teubner [1869], repr. 1894.

Rigler, A. *Examina Gymnasii Cliviensis publice indicit Fridericus Antonius Rigler, scholae director. Insunt annotationes maximam partem criticae in poetas Latinos, qui minores vocantur*. Cleves: Officina Kochiana, 1829 [Also contains the notes of C. A. M. Axt on the *Pervigilium*].

Rivinus, A. *Anonymi sed antiqui tamen poetae elegans et floridum carmen de vere, communiter Pervigilium Veneris inscriptum*. Leipzig and Frankfurt am Main: J. Pressius, 1644.

Robertson, D. S. 'The Date and Occasion of the Pervigilium Veneris'. *The Classical Review* 52, no. 3 (1938): 109–12.

Rollo, W. 'The Date and Authorship of the Pervigilium Veneris'. *Classical Philology* 24, no. 4 (1929): 405–08.

Romano, D. 'La genesi ed il significato del *Pervigilium Veneris* nella interpretazione di Walter Pater'. *Annali del Liceo classico G. Garibaldi di Palermo* 11–13 (1974–76): 289–95.

Rosati, G. 'Sabinus, the Heroides and the Poet–Nightingale. Some Observations on the Authenticity of the Epistula Sapphus'. *The Classical Quarterly* 46, no. 1 (1996): 207–16.

Sanadon, N.-É., *La traduction d'une himne sur les Fêtes de Vénus avec des remarques critiques sur la même pièce*. Paris: de la Roche, 1728.

Saumaise, C. Cl. *Salmasii Plininae exercitationes in Caii Iulii Solini Polyhistora*. Paris: C. Morellus, 1629.

Saumaise, C. Cl. *Salmasii Plininae exercitationes in Caii Iulii Solini Polyhistora*.[2] Utrecht: J. van de Water, J. Ribbius, F. Halma and G. van de Water, 1689.

Scaliger, J. – see Omont.

Schenkl, K. 'Zur Kritik des Pervigilium Veneris'. *Zeitschrift für die österreichischen Gymnasien* 18 (1867): 233–43.

Schilling, R. *La Veillée de Vénus. Pervigilium Veneris*. Paris: Les Belles Lettres, 1944.

Schilling, R. 'Une résurgence chrétienne du "Pervigilium Veneris" au 17ème siècle: l'Epinicium divini Amoris de Jacob Balde'. In: *Balde und Horaz*, edited by E. Lefèvre, K. Haß and R. Hartkamp, 375–9. Tübingen: Gunter Narr Verlag, 1999.

Schmitz, C. 'Warnung vor dem Liebesgott. Pervigilium Veneris, V. 56 credere oder cedere?' *Rheinisches Museum für Philologie* 149, no. 3–4 (2006): 359–68.

Schriverius, P. 'Animadvertiones in Pervigilium Veneris'. In: *Dominici Baudii Amores*, edited by Petrus Schriverius, 437–68. Leiden: Hegerus and Hackius, 1638.

Sedgwick, W. B. 'The Trochaic Tetrameter and the "Versus Popularis" in Latin'. *Greece & Rome* 1, no. 2 (1932): 96–106.

Shackleton Bailey, D. R. *Anthologia Latina I*. Stuttgart: Bibliotheca Teubneriana, 1982.

Shanzer, D. 'Once again Tiberianus and the Pervigilium Veneris'. *Rivista di Filologica e di Istruzione Classica* 118 (1990): 306–18.

Smolak, K. 'Pervigilium Veneris'. In: *Handbuch der lateinischen Literatur der Antike*, edited by R. Herzog and P. Lebrecht Schmidt, 258–63. Munich: C. H. Beck, 1989.

Stanley, T. *Europa. Cupid crucified. Venus' Vigils. With annotations, by Tho. Stanley Esq.* London: Printed by W.W. for Humphrey Moseley, 1649.

The pleasures of coition; or, the nightly sports of Venus: a poem. Being a translation of the Pervigilium Veneris, of the celebrated Bonefonius. With some other pieces. London: for E. Curll at the Dial and Bible, 1721.

Thill, A. 'La *Philomela* de Jacobus Balde. Création poétique dans une 'paraphrase' néolatine'. *Revue des études latines* 58 (1980): 428–48.

Thomas, P. Review: 'Pervigilium Veneris, Text en vertaling met inleiding en commentaar voorgezien door Dr. G. Brakman'. *Persée* 7, no. 3 (1928): 1065–06.

Traube, L. 'Zur lateinischen Anthologie'. *Philologus* 54 (1895): 124–35.

Trotski, J. 'Zum Pervigilium Veneris'. *Philologus* 81 (1926): 339–63.

Ussani, V. *In Pervigilium Veneris coniecturae*. Rome: Vogherae, 1896.

Valgiglio, E. 'Sulla tradizione manoscritta del *P.V.' Bolletino del Comitato per la preparazione dell'Edizione Nazionale dei Classici Greci e Latini* 'Accademia nazionale Lincei' 15 (1967): 115–35.

Wernsdorf, J. C. *Poetae Latini Minores.* 7 vols, vol. 3. Altenburg: Impensis Richteri, 1782.

Wilhelm, J. J. *The Cruelest Month: Spring, Nature and Love in Classical and Medieval Lyrics.* New Haven: Yale University Press, 1965.

Online resources

Declerq, D. *Pervigilium Veneris: La Veillée de Vénus, Traduction Nouvelle avec Notes.* Brussels: Université Catholique de Louvain, 2004. Available from: http://bcs.fltr.ucl.ac.be/PerVen/introduction.htm (last accessed 16 June 2017).

Salzman, P. et al. *Mary Wroth's Poetry: An Electronic Edition* (2012). Available from: http://wroth.latrobe.edu.au/index.html (last accessed 7 June 2017).

Further Reading

Chatelain, E. 'Sur le Pervigilium Veneris, II. Conjectures d'Achillius Statius'. *Revue de Philologie* 9 (1885): 127.

Duff, J. W. and A. M. Duff. *A Literary History of Rome in the Silver Age: From Tiberius to Hadrian*. 3rd edn. New York: Barnes and Noble, 1968.

Hersch, K. K. *The Roman Wedding: Ritual and Meaning in Antiquity*. Cambridge: Cambridge University Press, 2010.

Bibliography

Critical Poems

Appendix

Tiberianus 1 and 4: the *Amnis Ibat* and *Omnipotens*

1. *Amnis Ibat*[1]

Amnis ibat inter herbas, valle fusus frigida,
Luce ridens calculorum, flore pictus herbido.
Caerulas superne lauras et virecta myrtea
Leniter motabat aura blandiente sibilo.
Subtus autem molle gramen flore pulcro creverat:
Et croco solum rubebat et lucebat liliis.
Tum nemus fraglabat omne violarum spiritu.
Inter ista dona veris gemmeasque gratias
Omnium regina odorum vel colorum lucifer
Auriflora praeminebat, forma Dionis, rosa.
Roscidum nemus rigebat inter uda gramina:
Fonte crebro mumurabant hinc et inde rivuli,
Quae fluenta labibunda guttis ibant lucidis.
Antra muscus et virentes intus [hederae] vinxerant,
Has per umbras omnis ales plus canora quam putes
Cantibus vernis strepebat et susurris dulcibus:
Hic loquentis murmur amnis concinebat frondibus,
Quis melos vocalis aurae musa Zephyri, moverat.
Sic euntem per virecta pulchra odora et musica
Ales amnis aura lucus flos et umbra iuverat.

---

[1] Both texts follow the edition of F. Buecheler and A. Riese, *Anthologia Latina, sive Poesis latinae supplementum*. Vol 2. 2nd edn (Leipzig: Teubner, 1906). Poem 4, *Omnipotens*, is numbered 490 and poem 1, *Amnis ibat*, number 809 in his collection. The most recent edition of Tiberianus' poetry and fragments with an introduction and extensive notes is S. Mattiacci, *I carmi e i frammenti di Tiberiano: Introduzione, edizione critica, traduzione e commento* (Florence: Leo S. Olschki editore, 1990).

4. Omnipotens

Omnipotens, annosa poli quem suspicit aetas,
Quem sub millenis semper virtutibus unum
Nec numero quisquam poterit pensare nec aevo,
Nunc esto affatus, si quo te nomine dignum est,
Quo sacer ignoto gaudes, quod maxima tellus
Intremit et sistunt rapidos vaga sidera cursus.
Tu solus, tu multus item, tu primus et idem
Postremus mediusque simul mundique superestes:
Nam sine fine tui labentia tempora finis.
Altus ab aeterno spectans fera turbine certo
Rerum fata rapi vitasque involvier aevo
Atque iterum reduces supera in convexa referri,
Scilicet ut mundo redeat, quod partibus austrum
Perdiderit reluumque iterum per tempora fiat.
Tu, siquidem fas est in temet tendere sensum
Et speciem temptare sacram, qua sidera cingis
Immensus longamque simul complecteris aetheram,
Fulmineis forsan rapida sub imagine membris
Flammifluum quoddam iubar es, quo cuncta coruscans
Ipse vides nostrumque premis solemque diemque.
Tu genus omne deum, tu rerum causa vigorque,
Tu natura omnis, deus innumerabilis unus,
Tu sexu plenus toto, tibi nascitur olim
Hic deus, hic mundus, domus hic hominumque deumque,
Lucens, augusto stellatus flore iuventae.
Quem (precor, aspires), qua sit ratione creatus,
Quo genitus factusve modo, da nosse volenti.
Da, pater, augustas ut possim noscere causas,
Mundanas olim moles quo foedere rerum
Sustuleris animamque levi quo maximus olim
Texueris numero, quo congrege dissimilique,
Quicquid id est vegetum, quod per cita corpora vivit.

Index

Note: numbers in italic refer to occurrences of terms in the poem and translation.